Adelaide Kemble Sartoris

A week in a French country-house

Adelaide Kemble Sartoris

A week in a French country-house

ISBN/EAN: 9783337150532

Printed in Europe, USA, Canada, Australia, Japan

Cover: Foto ©Andreas Hilbeck / pixelio.de

More available books at **www.hansebooks.com**

A WEEK

IN A

FRENCH COUNTRY-HOUSE.

BY

ADELAIDE SARTORIS.

LONDON:
SMITH, ELDER AND CO., 65, CORNHILL.
1867.

TO DEAR MONSIEUR CHARLES AND MADAME OLYMPE,

IN MEMORY OF THE MANY HAPPY DAYS

PASSED AT MARNY-LES-MONTS.

A WEEK

IN A

FRENCH COUNTRY-HOUSE.

PART I.

"Here's a letter that concerns you, Bessy," said my mother one morning a week or two ago, as I came into our little breakfast-room at Linton.

"And we say you're to go," said aunt Emily.

"Oh, aunt Emily! go where?" I exclaimed in utter despair, and feeling ready to cry with fatigue at the bare idea of a move in any direction.

"Olympe has written," began my mother, holding up a thin letter with a yellow stamp upon it.

"Yes, and you are to go," once more broke in my impetuous old aunt Emily. The letter was from the Comtesse de Caradec, in answer to one from my poor dear mother, who it seems had been writing all her alarms about my health to her old friend and pupil; and now, as soon as I could get aunt Emily to promise silence, the letter was read out to me. It was cordial and affectionate, as all her letters are, and contained the kind proposal that I should go over to Marny-les-Monts, and try what a fortnight's entire change would do towards toning me up, and shaking me out of the languor, mental and physical, which had invaded me of late, and against which, for the first time in my life, I felt quite powerless to do battle.

The fact is, that my dear mother's illness, coming as it did, after a most exhausting term of hard work, had quite knocked me down. I had had a good many pupils and one or two schools also to attend during the last season; and the confinement of the life, together with the painful strain upon the nerves, which I suppose teaching music will always be to me, to the end of time, had already left me feeble and in want of rest, when mother was seized, first with bronchitis, then with inflammation of the lungs; and the terrible anxiety about her, combined with all those days spent in her hot room, and all those nights passed by her sick-bed, had prostrated me still farther. Then came our move down to aunt Emily's cottage in Devonshire, from which I had hoped wonders; but while it seemed to be bringing mother round beautifully, and making her quite fat and rosy again, I was dwindling away into an absolute shadow; I could not walk a step without violent palpitations; I fainted dead away after being out for ten minutes in the sun, and when aunt Emily spoke a little louder or sharper to me than usual, if it was only to say good morning, I began to cry. It was such a new state of things for me, that my two dear old guardian angels were getting quite troubled about me, and so after a good long discussion and many useless efforts on my part to persuade them to let me stay where I was and be quiet, it was finally decided that Madame de Caradec's kind invitation was to be accepted, and that I was to go abroad for the first time in my life, and see what entire change of air and scene would do for me.

Abroad! everything has been brought so close to one of late years by the increased rapidity of travelling, and every one is so continually on the move in consequence, that nothing short of

Australia, or the Himalayas, answers at all now to the important sound of the word "abroad." Italy, Germany, Switzerland, are become as familiar to everybody as Portman Square or Piccadilly, and my "abroad" meant even less than all this: a bit of France just off the high-road—no more—and within ten hours of England; it would take me very little longer to get there than it had taken us to come down to aunt Emily's.

Madame de Caradec's mother was an Englishwoman, but she herself was born in France, and married there, and has always lived there, both before and since her widowhood. Her only brother, who came to her when her husband died, and has remained with her ever since, I had heard of as entirely Anglomane in his tastes and habits. They buy English horses and keep English grooms, and I believe they even prefer English cookery; and she drives her own pony-chaise, and talks English better than I do. Oh, was it worth while to cross that horrid Channel, and no doubt be odiously ill, to go away from my own who love me, among a parcel of strangers, to find only another inferior sort of England? Oh, was it worth while? especially for a single week; for longer I was quite determined I would not stay? I did not say this, however, either to mother or to aunt Emily, for I saw that they had quite set their hearts on the project, and so I submitted with the best grace I was able to muster; saw my new carmelite, my best black silk, and a white muslin for evenings, put into my trunk, and finally, accompanied by old Margery, who had been with us ever since I was born, and who, having also once spent a single week in Paris when she was six years old, was considered likely to "be of use to me" on my journey, I took leave of my dear ones with a weary heart and watery eyes, and set forth upon my travels. I saw my dear mother with her slender figure, her silver hair, and sweet moonlight face, shading her eyes with her hand, and aunt Emily, who looked like a peony with a grizzled crop, both standing in the porch to look after us as long as we were in sight; but the turn in the road by the Angler's Home soon came, and hid us from each other, and then I felt fairly launched indeed and very desolate.

"Never mind, dear," said Margery, wiping a sympathetic drop from the tip of her pointed red nose. "I know *shpow* means hat."

We crossed on the 18th of October. It was a lovely day, and the steamer was crowded with passengers. It was too fine, and the sea too smooth, for any one to be ill, so I had the ladies' cabin all to myself, which I infinitely preferred to being in the midst of all those unfamiliar faces. I hitched myself up into a very comfortable berth, close to an open port-hole, through which I watched the great green swirls of water glittering in the sun, and the passage did not seem long. When we landed at Boulogne, the sky was so blue, the shops all looked so different; the fishwomen, with their short petticoats and their baskets on their backs, so curious; everything seemed so sparkling and unaccustomed, that I would not get into a carriage, but taking my bag in my hand walked with Margery the few steps from the boat to the station.

"Would you allow me, muddàm—porty-bag, muddàm?" said a voice at my side. I turned and recognized an Englishman, with a hot and anxious visage, who had just crossed over with us, and who was making for the same destination as ourselves.

"Thank you," I answered; "I can carry it quite easily; it's not at all heavy."

"Oh, Lord, mum!" ejaculated my friend with

effusion, "what a blessing it is to hear one's own language again!"

I felt inclined to advise him to venture no farther if he already experienced *mal du pays* to such an extent, but to go back and wait patiently at the pier until the next steamer started for England. We had two blooming young English ladies in our carriage, accompanied by a surly brother in one corner, who was far too satisfied with himself and too discontented with everything else not to have been a freeborn Briton. Just before arriving at the junction where Margery and I were to branch off from the great Paris main line for Marny-les-Monts, "Préparez vos billets, messieurs et mesdames, s'il vous plaît," said the conducteur.

"Stoopid ass!" remarked the Englishman, with sullen scorn; "in England they'd have said 'Tickets!' and there'd have been an end of it."

When we arrived at Hautbuisson (the station at which we had to get out), I found that the Countess had expected us by an earlier train, and had sent her carriage to meet us. Not finding us, however, it had gone home again, and we had to wait some time while another vehicle was being procured for us, so that it was already quite dark when we started for Marny-les-Monts—quite too dark to be able to see anything whatever of the scenery around us. I only felt that suddenly our road took us through the yet thicker black of trees; then again we emerged, and rolled and bumped with a muffled sound over a heavy wooden bridge; toiled up a sandy hill to the lights that were glimmering on the summit; heard a noise of loud voices and foreign tongues all vociferating together; and then I suddenly found myself lifted, I hardly knew how, out of the carriage, and into a tall and potent embrace, enveloped in which I was conveyed along, with my feet hardly reaching the ground, into a brilliant drawing-room. Here a tall gentleman bowed to me, who was presented to me as "my brother Charles." He turned with a kind anxiety to my conductress, and said, "Olympe, what will you do about the dinner?"

"She will dine in her own room," answered the Countess, with despotic melancholy.

"But perhaps she would rather come in with us at once, as we are still at table," he suggested, in a low voice.

"She will dine in her own room," repeated the Countess.

"Are you quite sure that you would like that best?" he again attempted, turning to me.

"She will dine in her own room," imperturbably remarked the Countess, without the slightest shade of difference in her intonation.

I was quite too shy to venture any opinion on the subject myself; moreover, I had an intuitive conviction that it was not expected of me: so, dazed with the sudden light and the new faces, and with the strong arm round me, I was carried, still upon the very tips of my toes, up the staircase, and finally deposited in a cheery little chintz bedroom, where, after a hearty kiss of welcome, I was left, much to my relief, to slip on my dressing-gown, put my feet up, and rest both the spirit and the flesh, which were equally tired out.

Presently, while Margery was arranging my things for the night, the cup of tea, which was all that I had asked for, was brought to me. As I lay with closed lids upon the sofa, I heard Margery say, "Here—on table—tray—put;" as if she thought that broken English, uttered in a very decisive manner, and with a break between each word, answered quite the same purpose as French.

"Does mademoiselle wish for anything else?" inquired the little maid.

"Toody swee," Margery observed, with perfect assurance.

"Do you speak French?" the little maid asked her, with a smile.

"Oh, wee," responded the undaunted Margery, adding "Shpow!" in what I thought rather a menacing way, as she kept nodding her head triumphantly at the girl, and giving sharp taps to her own bonnet, by way of convincing her then and there that she knew what was what.

Fortunately an Irish nurse, who had lived with Madame de Caradec ever since the birth of her daughter, just at this juncture arrived opportunely to the rescue, and Margery, having duly attended to my comfort, was borne off by her new friend to be made comfortable herself.

Later in the evening, just as I had finished writing to mother to tell her of my safe arrival, I heard a quick, decided step coming along the passage, and a hurried little tap at the door. "Come in," I said, and a charming child of about sixteen made her appearance. She was short for her age, but did not look so, from her erect carriage, and from the magnificent way in which her head was set upon her shoulders. She was brilliantly fair, with heaps of golden hair, which she wore turned back from her clear broad forehead. The charm of her face consisted in its great nobility. The expression was one of mixed decision and sweetness; and there was altogether a sort of veiled power about her, which, combined with her childish aspect, made her exceedingly attractive.

"Maman sends me to ask," she said in her sweet broken English, "will you more tea? or some sirop, perhaps? Have you, indeed, all you want?"

"I see you are Jeanne," said I, holding out my hands to her, and drawing her down on the sofa by my side.

"Yes, I am Jeanne," she replied in French. "I had been out with the hounds all day, and was late for dinner, and dressing in a hurry when you came; that was why you did not see me when you arrived. But Maman was there, I hope, and Charles, and René, to receive you?"

"I saw one gentleman in the drawing-room—your uncle Charles, I believe?"

"Yes," said Jeanne; "that was the Marquis."
"And who is René?" asked I.

"René is a cousin of Maman's, who comes here to hunt for three months every winter. De Saldes is his other name—René de Saldes. He always does what he pleases, and is never in time for anything. But the Marquis has to mind his *p*'s and *q*'s, or hm—hm!" and she screwed up her mouth and shook her head with a funny little sagacious expression.

"And you," said I, laughing, "are not obliged to mind your *p*'s and *q*'s, but come down when you like?"

"That depends," she answered. "When René comes out with us, I never get a scolding: there is a sort of complicated family machinery about it all, that it is a little difficult to understand at first. I protect the Marquis, and René protects me: not, indeed, that I need much protection; for they all of them spoil me very perfectly in their different ways, and Maman most of all, although she affects to bring me up with the utmost severity. But I must go now, for Maman desired me not to stay and tire you with my gossiping. I hunt to-morrow with our own hounds; but I shall have the pleasure of seeing you at breakfast before we go."

Then bidding me good-night, she left me to the enjoyment of the most perfect bed that ever rested weary limbs.

The next morning I was awoke by feeling something indescribably soft, cool, and fragrant touching my cheek ; and I opened my eyes into a large bunch of dewy, fresh-gathered roses. Madame Olympe was standing by my bedside with a heap of exquisite flowers in her hands, with which she proceeded to deck the jars on the chimney-piece and on the table.

She looked very grand and beautiful, enveloped from head to foot in a great white burnous, which fell in thick heavy folds round her stately person, and was altogether a most satisfactory morning vision, with the white hood over her head shading and softening her stern face, as she bent over her many-coloured treasures and arranged them silently. When she had filled the vases, she came and sat down on the foot of my bed.

" How are you," she said, " after your journey ? rested ? It was much better for you to dine in your own room—you would have felt shy and uncomfortable the first evening with strangers."

"Have you people staying with you now?" I inquired.

"Yes: we have René de Saldes, Monsieur Kiowski, and Monsieur Berthier. The first is my cousin, the last two are painter friends of mine. They will amuse you, they make such a contrast to each other. The one is so rapid in everything he does, and the other so slow. When they come together their differences not only appear more pronounced, but actually become so. They act unconsciously upon each other, and Monsiur Kiowski rushes on like a small millstream, while Monsieur Berthier takes an hour to say the slightest thing. I am also expecting some time to day Lady Blankeney and her daughter, and Miss Hamilton."

"My dear Madame Olympe," said I, "I should never have had the courage to come if I had thought to find so many people here."

"Oh," she answered, "you needn't feel at all alarmed, : there is only one person to be frightened at in the whole lot, and that is Miss Hamilton. Lady Blankeney is only a harmless, silly sort of little old fly: if you will but let her flutter and buzz, she will be quite content; she does all the talking herself. I rather like it and never think of answering her; and Maria is the quietest of the quiet, and properest of the proper —pure English growth—a bashful, blushing, infantile old maid of nine-and-thirty—the thing don't exist with us. They are both great bores, and I am sorry they should happen to be coming just in this particular time, because I should have liked you to become acquainted with René de Saldes, and he is already gone; knowing they were to be here to-day, he fled early in the morning. I am rather curious to see how they will make it out with Ursula Hamilton; she must startle Lady Blankeney occasionally, I should think."

"What is the tie between them? Is she any relation of theirs?" I inquired.

"There is a sort of distant cousinship," answered Madame Olympe. "Miss Hamilton's father had once a good fortune, which he squandered in every conceivable discreditable way, and then went to live for economy, with his little girl, at Florence. He died some time ago, and Ursula was left all but destitute. She then, to the horror of all her friends, announced her intention of going on the stage, for which, it appears, she has an immense natural talent—when suddenly, by the greatest piece of unlooked-for good luck in the world, a rich old aunt of hers died, and bequeathed her a very large sum of money. So, thank goodness, she gave up (though I do believe it was rather *à contre cœur*) the notion of singing in public, and Lady Blankeney, who had been in Italy during all her troubles, and carefully ignored both her and them, flew to her the instant she became an heiress, and is now convoying her to England, where she means to have the honour and glory of producing the new lioness in fashionable society. I own I'm rather curious to see them together, for ages ago I used to hear about Ursula Hamilton from my cousin, Monsieur de Saldes, who knew her abroad, and she appeared to be anything but an amenable subject, although at that time she was only fifteen or sixteen. But I shall leave you to dress now—you needn't hurry, for we don't breakfast till half-past eleven."

With that she nodded her head in a friendly way, and strode majestically out of the room.

I had been so thoroughly roused by Madame Olympe's visit, that I got up as soon as she had left me. I unfastened those delicious French windows that open from top to bottom, and seem to let all heaven and earth at once into the room, threw back the outer jalousies, and feasted my eyes upon the landscape. Before me lay the park (a bit of land redeemed from the heart of the forest, and cleared for the dwelling of my hostess) dotted all over with clumps of trees: here and there little screens of delicate young poplars, already turned by the season, quivered their golden leaves in the clear splendours of the autumn blue. At the bottom of the hill lay the river, of which my room commanded three different views as it turned and wound about, all glittering and rippling, and covered, as it were, with an ever-vibrating network of light; and beyond, stretching up and on for miles and miles around us, was the great ocean of the forest, drenched in deep dews, steeped in warm sunshine, swaying in the sweet morning freshness, and chanting its solemn hymn of gladness to the Lord of all the beauties of the earth.

When I was dressed, I went into the drawing-room, where I found Madame Olympe, still in the same picturesque costume, assiduously dusting the books upon the table with a feather brush. "This is not much like England after all," thought I.

"We have a new servant," she said in a plaintive tone of voice, "who never touches a thing in the morning, and so I am obliged to go round myself and see to it."

"Why, what does she do?" I inquired; "lie in bed till this hour?"

"The she is a he, whose name is Hyacinthe, and that is what he does!" she answered, pointing with her brush to the chandelier.

I looked up; it was a quaint edifice, built entirely of stags' heads and antlers carved in wood, and it was filled from top to bottom with flowers and leaves grouped together in the loveliest way.

"Look there—and there," she said.

I glanced round the room; in every corner there were heaps and heaps of flowers arranged, with every variety of sword-like rush and feathery plume of grass.

"Would you like to see the artist himself? There he is!" she continued, opening the door which led out into the hall. Beyond the hall was a large portico, fitted up with sofas and chairs, and here, at a table covered with flowers, sat a short fat man with a turn-up nose, pasty face, and sentimental aspect, dressing a couple of huge vases. These he afterwards brought in and placed triumphantly upon the chimney-piece; they were entirely filled with the most delicate ferns, intermingled with dark ivy-leaves, which fell over and round the jars in garlands of exquisite grace.

At breakfast I was introduced to Monsieur Berthier, a gentleman who looked about fifty-five years old. He was fair, rather bald, and had the gentlest voice and manner in the world. He very kindly endeavoured to put me at my ease by speaking to me in English, but his pronunciation was so peculiar that I could hardly understand what he said—which made me much more nervous than I was before. However, they all soon found out that I spoke French without difficulty, and then we got on swimmingly.

Monsieur Charles appeared in full hunting costume. He did not wear the green, which is the colour of the Imperial hunt, but a white coat with maroon velvet facings: it was extremely picturesque, and very becoming to pretty little Jeanne, who was charmingly got up in the same colours.

They called this morning meal their breakfast, but it was to all intents and purposes a regular dinner. There were two large dishes of hot meat, two or three others of cold, hot dressed vegetables, salad, eggs, and all served upon the bare oak table without any table-cloth. At the end where Madame Olympe sat, were the urn and breakfast-service; but I observed that everybody drank wine-and-water to begin with, and then gradually arrived at tea as a sort of climax, when a most delicious hot heavy pastrycake was handed round, which they ate with an addition of butter and honey that made me expect to see them die on their chairs by my side. It is but fair to add that this breakfast and their dinner are the only meals partaken of in the day. The servants have their breakfast and dinner immediately after their masters have done, upon what is left; the whole domestic machinery seems to me much simpler than our English arrangements. French servants do not eat or drink half so much as ours do, and make much fewer difficulties. What complicates matters in England a good deal is the separate life led by the children : this does not exist in France, where the children keep for the most part the same hours with their parents, instead of dining apart and early, as ours do.

While we were in the middle of breakfast a figure darted past the window, gesticulating violently—this I found was Monsieur Kiowski, who had been out painting and had not heard the breakfast-bell. Presently he rushed in with his sketch-book in his hand : he was quite young, and very pleasant-looking.

"Mille pardons!" he said, hurrying up to Madame Olympe and kissing her hand. "I hadn't any idea it was so late, but I found the most adorable little bit to paint from the boat-house! When first I got there it was all cool greys and silver tones—a perfect Corot—with just that little bit of dead tree coming in there you see" (showing her the book) " to give it a red accent ; but when the sun came out the whole aspect altered from minute to minute, so that I was obliged to give it up at last. I must try and get up early again to morrow to finish it if possible. Good-morning, Jeanne. Good-morning, Marquis. Good-morning, Berthier. Why didn't you come out and have a go at the river too? You have no idea how lovely it looked from the inside of the boat-house; but perfectly adorable!" (and he sent a kiss into the air rapturously from the tip of his fingers). "Yes, some *pommes de terre sautées*, Hyacinthe, if you please."

All this came pelting out in a torrent of French, and in a single breath, and I was perfectly dumfoundered when Madame Olympe presented him to me, and he asked me in equally faultless English if I had had a good night and was rested after my journey?

"Mademoiselle does not look as if she had crossed the sea yesterday: were you ill?" asked Monsieur Berthier in his slow gentle way. "I think the English character never comes out more strongly than on board a steamboat," he continued. "The feeling of *decency—le convenable—* is what English people never lose sight of— English women more especially: even the tortures of sea-sickness they manage to control, and retire to some secluded corner with their basin, hoping to shroud from observation an attitude which no amount of will can render graceful or dignified. I saw a vulgar Spaniard once, when I was crossing over to England : he had been making game of a poor Meess, who, with English forethought, had provided herself with a basin before the vessel started. He straddled about on deck with a great chain and a gaudy cane, and said in a swaggering way, 'Look at all these poor wretches who are determined to be ill! Their precautions are exactly what makes them so; they are afraid, and give in, and of course are sick immediately; but if one walks up and down as I do, and smokes as I do, and sings as I do, one is never ill.' He began executing some roulades as the boat steamed out of harbour; the sea was terrible, and before ten minutes were over, my Spaniard, who had suddenly lapsed into ominous silence and gradually become of a hue the like of which I never beheld before or since on any human countenance, uttered a discordant shriek, and made a violent plunge at a basin he saw upon a bench near him—the ship lurched, the basin rolled off, and he rolled after it and lay wallowing there on the ground where he fell, an utterly demoralized and disgusting object; but so miserable and so regardless of all appearances that I assure you he became almost grand through excess of suffering, and the entire absence of self-consciousness. Meess, with her basin in her corner, and all her British dignity, was *little* by the side of that Spaniard in the agony of his utter self-abandonment."

We all laughed, but Madame Olympe took the English side of the question and stood up for it very vigorously. Monsieur Berthier turned to me.

"Confess that you went downstairs and tried to hide yourself from every one; you would not be English if you had not done this. I remember at one time of my life having to pass every day the English pastrycook's at the corner of the Rue de Rivoli. I used to see the English Misses there eating cakes, and when I looked in at the window at them (for they were almost always pretty) they took a crumb at a time, but when I passed on, and they thought they were not seen any more, they put enormous pieces into their mouths, and ate with as much voracity as other people. I used to amuse myself with pretending to go by, and then coming back stealthily to watch them from the corner of the window, and they always did the same."

"Well," said Monsieur Kiowski, "and very right too: you seem to think it ridiculous and unpoetical, but after all, it shows a regard for the feelings of others, and a certain sense of beauty too, which in my humble opinion are qualities rather than defects."

André now came to say that the horses were at the door, and we all went out upon the perron to see them start. Jeanne embraced her mother, and the Marquis kissed his sister's hand before they mounted. The horses were English, and very handsome beasts, and the Marquis's tall slight figure in his gay uniform, and with his great hunting-horn slung over his shoulder, looked uncommonly well as they passed in and out through the trees, with the sun shining full upon them. How I envied them their ride,—I, who could not even walk!

"I am sorry I cannot drive you to the meet to-day," said Madame Olympe to me, "because these people are coming. However, you must see it one day before you go; it is very different from the English hunting, but it is very pretty in the forest, and we can follow it perfectly in a carriage and see all the sport."

While we were still standing on the perron watching the receding figures as they went down the hill, we saw a little black object with a white head-dress flitting swiftly towards the house. As she came nearer to us, I saw that it was a Sister of Charity.

"It is the Sœur Marie," said Madame Olympe, going forward to meet her. "The school-children are under her direction and she is the good angel of the neighbouring village. Good-morning, my sister. Are you come to see me about the school-feast, or to tell me of some of your poor people who want help? Will you not come in and have some breakfast?"

"Oh, no, Madame la Comtesse," said the little sister. "I breakfasted long ago; besides, I must not eat such dainty things as you would give me in your goodness: my wicked body must be mortified, and I must keep a tight rein over the sinful appetites of the flesh."

We could hardly help laughing at this speech proceeding from the mouth of the poor sister.

Sœur Marie.

She was a spare, small old creature, mere skin and bone, with a pale, childish, toothless face, small brown watery eyes, and a feeble beseeching voice. Her whole figure had something eager, anxious, and imploring, in its expression, and her quick gait and restless activity, combined with the flutter of her draperies, and a way she had of leaning slightly forward, always somehow gave her the appearance of flying.

"Well, but a glass of wine and a little bit of cake, my sister—at least that after your long walk? Surely that comes under the head of necessary sustenance?"

"No, no, my dear lady," answered the little sister, with childish earnestness; "I must wrestle with temptation, and overthrow my rebellious passions."

"And why are you not more warmly clad, Sœur Marie?" continued Madame Olympe. "The day is treacherous—warm in the sun and cold in the shade. What have you done with the woollen handkerchief I gave you to keep those little bones of yours warm?"

"Oh, Madame la Comtesse must not be angry," said the little creature, looking imploringly up in her face, "but old Nanon has had her rheumatism so badly of late, that I gave it to her. Madame knows how I value her kindness, but the poor Nanon was so suffering, and, for the moment, I really had no use for it."

"That is always the way," said Madame Olympe, turning to me; "she never keeps anything for herself. However, I do hope that the india-rubber bottle which you brought over for me will be of some comfort to her during the winter; perhaps, as that is neither food nor clothing, I may be able to persuade her to keep it."

She then sent for one of those india-rubber bags which she had begged me to bring from England for her, and when the servant had fetched it she gave it to the old sister saying, "Here, my sister, is something to make you comfortable in the winter."

Sœur Marie took it with overflowing gratitude, but evidently without having the slightest idea what was to be done with it, or how it was to be made use of. Madame Olympe watched her for a minute or two, and then, finding that she was too timid and humble to make any inquiry, she proceeded to explain to her the method of unscrewing it, putting in the hot water, and screwing it up again. Sœur Marie was in an ecstasy of delight.

"There!" said Madame Olympe. "On cold winter nights, when it is full of nice hot water, and you are in bed, my sister, you see you can clap it here—or here—or here—or just wherever you please!" and she whisked it about all over her own body as she spoke, with a droll unconsciousness, and a dear, benevolent beaming face, quite unlike any expression I had thought her countenance capable of. It was charming to see her unbend so completely, and become so sweet and tender to the poor flittering little nun.

Presently they went in together, to talk over a feast that Madame de Caradec was going to give the school-children, and Monsieur Berthier and I went strolling slowly round the house.

It was quite the most enjoyable dwelling I ever was in: I believe, from the fact that it was entirely devoid of any pretension to architectural importance. Wherever a pretty view or sunny aspect invited one to sit, and look or bask, as the case might be, great wide balconies had been thrown out, with awnings moveable at pleasure;

in other places, there were cool verandahs, with seats, for those who preferred the shade. I expressed my approbation of the exterior of the house to Monsieur Berthier. Just then a jalousie was thrown vehemently open, and Monsieur Kiowski's head appeared at the window above us.

"You have delicious weather for your little walk," he remarked to me, with great urbanity; then in French to Monsieur Berthier,—"I envy you, mon cher, you who are able to enjoy your holiday in peace."

"I think I have some little right to enjoy it," returned the other; "I have earned it by working hard enough, I am sure. I was grinding away at the wheel until the very last moment before I came here."

"But at all events," said Monsieur Kiowski, "when you have done, you have done. Monsieur has given his lessons, Monsieur walks, Monsieur talks, Monsieur takes his leisure; while I, after working like a galley-slave in order to get the underpainting of my picture done before coming over, have brought with me two drawings, which I am absolutely obliged to finish by the end of this week, besides any quantity of letters which I have always delayed answering, from a futile idea that I should find time at Marny-les-Monts for everything I wanted to do. What a lovely day it is!" He then again said to me in English,— " How I should like to come down and bask in the sun ! "

" Why don't you come? what is it that you are doing at the present moment?" I asked rather satirically.

"Writing my letters," he answered with perfect naïveté, leaning his arms upon the window-sill and looking out at us.

" Well," said Monsieur Berthier, as we walked on, " and the interior of the house ? You do not say what impression that makes upon you ? "

" I have been here such an instant of time," I answered, " that I hardly dare trust my own impressions. How striking little Jeanne is ! She seems to me like a clasped book : if ever I get the clasps open I'm sure that I shall like what I shall read ; but she is not easy to know, and I should think did not readily attach herself to strangers. However, she is exactly what I expected to find her, from all her mother had written about her to my mother."

"And Madame de Caradec," he continued, "is she also what you expected to find her?"

"No," said I, laughing, "for I was told that she was rather imposing, and I find her positively alarming, and I was told that she had been handsome and I think her perfectly beautiful still—don't you?"

"I see that you are very impressionable," he said, smiling at my enthusiasm, "but of course I see her differently who have known her from her childhood. Ah! that first youth! how beautiful it is! It has a charm—a mystery—so soon lost, and that nothing afterwards, however fine, can compensate for!—at least such is my opinion. You think her beautiful now: then just imagine what she must have been at sixteen, when I first knew her. She was a famous beauty then, I assure you! You know I was her drawing-master, and I shall never forget the day that I gave her her first lesson. I went there never yet having seen her, and I was perfectly bewildered (I too was young then) when I beheld this vision of heavenly beauty before me! Madame your mother was sitting working in the room at the time. I knew her very well—Madame Hope and I were great friends."

A Story of Disappointed Love.

"I have constantly heard mother say so," said I, "and it has been a real delight to me to come among the people I have so often heard her speak of with affection. But did Madame de Caradec always look as proud and sad as she does now?" I inquired.

"No," answered Monsieur Berthier. "That expression came with trouble and with time: it dates back to an old story of disappointed attachment. Did Madame Hope never mention Monsieur Hamilton to you?" he asked, after a slight pause. "He used to come to the house a great deal during the time that she was in France. Well, it was for him that Madame de Caradec once had a very profound sentiment. He made no sign, however, of any corresponding feeling, beyond seeming to admire her very much; so much, indeed, that everybody was quite surprised that he did not come forward and offer to marry her, but he did not, and it was then that she first began to look proud and hard. She remained single—courted, followed, and adored as she was, until she was seven-and-twenty; and then, to the amazement of every one, as you may conceive, she suddenly chose from among all her suitors the old

D

Comte de Caradec, who was at least sixty when she accepted him. He was a charming old man, and very fond and proud of her, and I think she might have been happy, or at all events tolerably contented with her life, if unluckily at her father's death (which took place seven or eight years after she was married) she had not found amongst his papers a letter from her old love, declaring his feeling for her, and containing a proposal of marriage. They had kept it from her —never consulted her—never even given her the little comfort of knowing that he had really cared for her. After this discovery, she had a long dangerous illness, through which her poor old husband nursed her with the tenderest devotion; but though through his care she eventually recovered, everything like happiness was at an end, and she became at once and for ever the stern melancholy woman that you see her now."

"And what became of Colonel Hamilton?" I inquired, eagerly.

"Oh, the brilliant colonel went abroad and ran away with an Italian prima donna, who died soon after, leaving him an only daughter: that is the Miss Hamilton who is coming to-day. I shall be very glad to see her again—I used to see a great deal of her at Florence."

"What sort of man was Colonel Hamilton?" said I. "Were you acquainted with him?"

"Yes," answered Monsieur Berthier. "He passed a considerable portion of his time in Paris; but I own he always appeared to me to be perfectly uninteresting."

"Was he handsome?" said I.

"He was thought so in the fashionable world," he replied; "and I have observed that that is a thing which always goes a very long way with your sex; they seldom have the courage to admire what is not generally admired by the women of their acquaintance. I confess I thought him rather insignificant-looking myself; he used to dress in the most exaggerated height of the fashion, and always looked as if he had just walked out of the *Journal des Modes.*"

"But," said I, "surely there must have been something remarkable about him to make a woman of that character care for him so much. Was he clever in any way, or amusing?"

"No," answered Monsieur Berthier; "he was dull, unoriginal, and commonplace; and I own I never myself could understand the attraction he had for her." Here he paused and looked at the landscape, and then added with a gentle sigh,— " Perhaps she had seen him in his uniform."

We were passing once more under Monsieur Kiowski's window, and he popped out his head again.

" Have you been as far as the stables, Miss Hope?" he inquired.

I told him that I had not yet, whereupon he addressed Monsieur Berthier.

" Monsieur Berthier, have you seen the stables since you have been here this time? There is a Virginia creeper already turned crimson, growing up the wall, and all over the roof, which is too wonderfully beautiful! That crimson against the stone-colour, and the red of the leaf upon the red of the tiles, make the most divine harmony I ever beheld!"

"Will you go and see it?" said Monsieur Berthier to me.

I was beginning to feel rather tired, so I declined.

" I advise you to go and see that, mon cher," continued Monsieur Kiowski; "it is marvellously fine. There," he said, craning his neck out of the window, until I was afraid he would fall. "When I stretch out like that, I just get a corner of the foliage gleaming like rubies against the blue sky." He then held up his hand to try the value of the flesh-coloured tone against the light, and added to me—"What a delicious air, to be sure! *un venticello che consola!* I really think I must come down."

"Why don't you?" said I, once more. "Are you working very hard at the present moment?"

"*Hélas!*" said he, with a sigh.

"What at?" asked I.

"At one of my drawings," he answered quite seriously.

"Do tell me," I inquired of Monsieur Berthier, "of what nation Monsieur Kiowski is?"

"English," he replied; "of Polish origin, I fancy, but his family is English, and so is he."

"Is not his French quite wonderful?" said I.

"Yes," he answered, "but not more so, I believe, than his Italian and German. I have heard Germans say they should have taken him for a German."

"Ah! imagine what happens to me!" screamed

Madame Olympe from the house; "such a telegram from Lady Blankeney!"

She hurried out in fits of laughter, with the paper in her hand. It was as follows:—

"Lady Blankeney, Hôtel Bristol, Paris, to Madame la Comtesse de Caradec, à Marny-les-Monts, près Champenay, Oise. Dearest Countess —in despair—we bring a fiddler—too dreadful— so shocked—pardon."

"One of Ursula's queer artist friends evidently," said Madame Olympe, "or Lady Blankeney would not have thought it necessary to apologize: some ill-combed genius that she has picked up abroad and brought along with her, no doubt. The question is, where on earth I am to lodge him? I haven't a corner to spare; I have been obliged to put Madame Simon, the housekeeper, who is ill, into Jeanne's room, in order to give her more air; and Jeanne already sleeps with me. There would be René's room, but then he is so uncertain that I never dare make use of it—he might get bored in Paris, you know," turning to Monsieur Berthier, "and come back at any moment. There's no use in telegraphing back to say I can't take the fiddler in, for they must

A Difficulty Surmounted.   39

already have started. Monsieur Kiowski only goes away on Wednesday; what on earth am I to do?"

"Dear Madame Olympe," said I, "do pray make some use of my room. I see that there is a sofa-bed in it; why shouldn't you put Miss Blankeney or Miss Hamilton into my bed and let me sleep on that? You know the *cabinet de toilette* affords every sort of convenience for double dressing."

This was an obvious arrangement to propose. My room was large and cheery, with only the bed in it to prevent it from looking like a pretty sitting-room, and beyond, opening into it, there was another smaller room, with all the washing and dressing appurtenances kept completely to themselves.

"You save my life!" said Madame Olympe. "Miss Blankeney is frightened to death if she is not quite close to her mother; but Ursula was to have had the little room next to yours. We will stick the fiddler in there, and put Ursula up with you, since you are good enough to have her. She shall sleep on the sofa, though—I won't have you turned out of your comfortable bed for any one. And now come in, for you are looking quite exhausted, and you must put your feet up upon the sofa."

She took me in, and established me, in spite of the feeble remonstrance I ventured to make, upon a wonderful sort of gigantic double sofa that stood in the drawing-room, midway between the fireplace and an oriel window, which commanded a lovely view of the river and the forest. She arranged the pillows for me, and then went out into the hall and brought back a soft shawl, with which she wrapped my feet round as tenderly as mother would, looking all the while so grand, and stately, and abstracted, that I was quite confused, and felt as though I were being waited upon by some great queen.

She went to the piano, opened it, and began one of Beethoven's sonatas. She played with a good deal of power and feeling, and with an evident love of her subject. I listened in enchantment. Monsieur Berthier took a book and sat down in a corner, but I saw that he was looking from underneath his eyebrows much oftener at her than at his book.

While she was still playing, a carriage drove

up to the door, and Lady Blankeney was announced. I was going to get up from the sofa, when Madame Olympe, who had left the piano, put me down again with a strong arm, saying in an imperative voice, "Don't move! don't move!" held me there steadily till the whole party had entered the room. First came a short thin old lady, fashionably dressed in a brown gown and pink bonnet; then a tall woman in a complete travelling suit of greys, with fair hair and projecting teeth, and then a young lady with a sallow face and large black eyes: she was dressed in black, and was closely followed by a little pale miserable-looking mortal, muffled from head to foot in a long great-coat, and with a huge comforter rolled two or three times round his throat.

"How d'ye *do*, dear Madame de Caradec! How d'ye *do!* Here we all are at last! Is that the princess?" she said, in a low voice, looking at me; "so delightful to find her still here! Pray present me. I shall be so charmed to make her acquaintance!"

"It isn't the princess," said Madame Olympe, rather drily; "it's only Miss Hope, my old governess's daughter." At which piece of information all the smiles vanished in an instant from Lady Blankeney's countenance, and she looked carefully in another direction.

"Miss Hamilton," said Madame Olympe, going up to the young lady in black, " I am glad to see you at Marny."

"And I to be here," answered a full contralto voice, with a remarkably distinct utterance. "This is Monsieur Dessaix," she continued, introducing her friend. "He has come all the way from Germany to see me, and if I had not brought him along with me, I must have stayed behind myself, so I hope you will forgive the liberty I have taken."

Madame Olympe bowed slightly, and so did the little man. He and Miss Hamilton were standing close together at the head of the sofa, and presently I heard him say to her in a low querulous voice,—

" My angel, I am suffocating!"

"Take off your comforter then, you stupid old owl," she answered, in a whisper.

"It will have a much better air if I wait till I go upstairs——but I am suffocating!"

"Then suffocate," she said, and went off into a giggle.

"Do not laugh, I entreat of thee," he continued; "thou wilt make me ridiculous before all these people; thy young friend with the teeth detests me already; if she could kill me she would. Well! what is going to be done now?" he continued, looking round with a discontented air; "is everybody going away? Ah, pour l'amour de Dieu, ne me laisse pas seul avec la morte!" This last was said in a sudden agonized whisper, as he saw Miss Hamilton preparing to follow the other ladies out of the room, but his terror made it quite audible, and the "morte" could not help laughing too. They then all went out together to take a turn in the grounds, and I remained lying on my sofa, rather tired, a little puzzled, and very much diverted.

I lay there and thought my thoughts, and looked out at the forest, and the river, and the sky, and as the time drew on I saw the water grow blood-red with the reflection of sunset clouds, and the trees grow darker and darker in the clear heavens, until at last they stood cut out in a thousand delicate and fantastic shapes in perfect black against the golden evening air. Then all the various hues melted and deepened together into one strange passionate amber twilight; a magical sound of horns playing in concert came dimly up out of lost distances, then a pleasant noise of voices and of horses' hoofs coming slowly up the hill, and presently Jeanne made her appearance followed by Hyacinthe and the lamp, and all the dreams vanished away with the bright light.

They had had famous sport and she was in high spirits. "You mustn't let me dawdle and chatter too long," she said, as she came and sat on a footstool by the side of the sofa, "or I shall be late for dinner again. The Marquis wanted badly to take a walk in the garden, but Maman has sent him to his room to get ready, and I must be in time too, as we have no René to-day to fall back upon."

"Are you sorry he is gone?" said I.

"I believe so!" was the emphatic answer.

"Tell me about him," said I. "What is he like? At all like your uncle Charles?"

She laughed. "Oh, no! nothing was ever more different. Why, Charles is not at all handsome—at least I suppose people wouldn't think him so, though I like his looks. His features are not particularly good I daresay; but he has a distinguished air for all that, which I care for a great deal more. Now about René there cannot be two opinions; he is simply magnificent."

Her funny little decided manner made me smile. "And what is he besides—amiable and kind?"

"No," said Jeanne; "he is certainly not amiable, and I am not quite sure that he is very kind. It is my poor Marquis that is all this. He does himself so little justice, and is so simple and unpretending, that one has to live with him before one finds out all the goodness that he keeps hidden away under a bushel. His kindness to the poor is inconceivable, and his courtesy of manner to them—I never saw any one with such delicate consideration as he has for all those who are in an inferior position to himself. Then no one is so sincere as he, or of such scrupulous niceness in all matters of honour; and as for his tact, it is unequalled, and would alone render him easy and agreeable to live with. René, at bottom, rather looks down upon him. René is travelled, and learned, and artistic, and interesting—above all, interesting; that is the very word for him. But he never thinks much about anybody, that I can see, except himself: and yet somehow, I don't know why, one can't help having a feeling of immense respect for him; I suppose, because he has always the air of despising one so—it gives one immediately a morbid desire after his approbation and notice. It is a great thing for us to have him come here in the winters; we should fall back into the benighted state of the middle ages, and do nothing but kill our hogs and eat them, if it were not for him! He keeps us all up to the mark. I always read up to him when he is coming, and we never dare shut an eye of an evening; and Maman dresses herself properly, and puts on no more gowns that were made in the year one; and Charles does not make any dirty jokes; and even the cook sends up superhuman dinners when he is at Marny! Do you understand him at all from my description?"

"I am afraid," I answered, "that what I do understand I should not very much like."

"Oh, you couldn't help liking him!" she interrupted. "One must feel drawn to him when he smiles his little tired smile, and looks sadly at one with those charming eyes of his."

"Why does he look unhappy?" I inquired; "has he had troubles?"

"O dear, no!" said Jeanne; "he has always been very prosperous. Maman says he is sad because he has always his own way; but yet she, like every one else, gives it to him. The Marquis fights, and struggles, and contends, and always goes to the wall, repulsed with loss; while with René it is just the reverse—he never discusses, and never submits."

The clock struck half-past seven, and we hurried upstairs. I went into my *cabinet de toilette*, which possessed a door giving into the corridor, as well as the one opening into the bedroom, and dressed for dinner, leaving the larger room for Miss Hamilton. I made haste, and got down before she did, and was sitting in the drawing-room with the others when she came in.

I was perfectly amazed at the transformation that dress and lamplight made in her. I had thought her all but plain on her arrival; now she appeared to me one of the most striking-looking persons I had ever seen. All the positive beauty of the face lay in the upper part. Large dark powerful eyes with heavy lids, almost always half-closed, gave her a most peculiar expression. Her eyelashes were the longest and thickest I ever beheld. They curled up at the ends, and stood out beyond her nose, as one looked at her in profile. Her eyebrows were coal-black and perfectly straight, and lay like a bar across her broad pale forehead, on which great masses of crisp black hair grew very low. She had a small, delicately shaped nose, with sensitive nostrils; her upper lip was too long, and her mouth, which was thin, had a perpetual sarcastic motion, which was strange, and not agreeable, in one so young. Her complexion was bad, and she had little or no colour; but the skin, which looked yellow and dingy in the morning, became a sort of wonderful cream-colour by candle-light. Her figure was perfectly magnificent, and there was a picturesqueness in all her movements which made it a delight to be in the room with her. I suppose I should have thought her tall in any other house, for she told me that she was five foot seven; but Madame Olympe was five foot ten, and anyhow no one had a chance of looking tall where she was.

The dinner went off well, and was extremely amusing. There had been a slight difficulty about the order of our going in. Of course Monsieur Charles had to take in Lady Blankeney; Madame Olympe then said, "Where is Monsieur Dessaix? He was here not a minute ago."

Monsieur Dessaix looked about forty; he was at all events considerably older than Monsieur Kiowski. He therefore was to have been Miss Blankeney's partner; but just at the moment that he was called for by Madame Olympe, I saw him stoop down and hide behind a large arm-chair, from which place of refuge, as soon as he saw Monsieur Kiowski invested with his honours and conveying the fair Maria safely in to dinner, he emerged, and quietly offered his arm to Ursula. Jeanne and I went in together, leaving Monsieur Berthier for Madame Olympe. Fortunately her head had been turned the other way, and I don't think any one but Miss Hamilton and I were the wiser for the manœuvre which had just been performed.

"Dost thou find me changed since thou sawest me last?" said Monsieur Dessaix to Miss Hamilton, with a melancholy air.

The table was round and the party small, so

that every one was more or less within earshot of all that passed. I saw the sharp look of amazed disapprobation which came over Madame Olympe's face as, for the first time, the *thee* and *thou* which had surprised me, attracted her attention. I saw that she was riveted—evidently for a moment thinking that she must have heard amiss; but the answer did not keep us long waiting—it came ringing out distinctly in Miss Hamilton's grave tones :—

"What change dost thou expect me to find in thee, Jacques? Thy hair has not turned white in five weeks' time."

"No," said he; "but it has fallen off dreadfully during those five weeks. Dost thou see how bald I am becoming?"

"I have observed," said Monsieur Berthier to me, "that men become bald much more frequently than women. One can hardly enter a room where there are a few persons assembled, without seeing some man with a bald head. If you look round the table here, you will see that out of the four male heads present there are three already bald : Monsieur Charles, Monsieur Dessaix, and myself. Of course there must be some reason for a fact which there is no disputing, and I have always attributed it to the work of thought which goes continually on in the brain of man."

"Ah, my old enemy!" cried Ursula, from the other side of the table. "We don't think, don't we?"

"No, I do not quite say that," he answered, laughing gently; "but you will allow that women's thoughts are generally occupied with less weighty considerations; much of the child's nature enters into the composition of woman. And note well that this is no accusation; on the contrary, it is one of your greatest charms, in my opinion, and it is that quality which gives you the power of relaxing and reposing the mind of man when it is weary with solving the serious problems of life."

"Belle vocation!" said she, and down went the corners of her mouth. "As for the problems of life, not to me, nor to you either, will it be given to solve them, my dear Berthier."

"Monsieur Dessaix, what will you eat?" asked Madame Olympe, seeing that his plate was empty.

"Some of that little corpse if you please, Madame la Comtesse," he answered feebly, pointing to a fowl that looked very white in the middle of brown gravy.

Jeanne gave one wild compressed look at Monsieur Charles, hastily seized some water, and exploded in her glass with a tremendous noise.

"I am not laughing—I am not laughing—I am not laughing," said Madame Olympe, with menacing sternness.

"I perceive," said I, turning to Monsieur Berthier, "that you think us greatly inferior to men."

"Don't talk to him, Miss Hope," said Ursula; "he has the worst opinion of us. Oh, I know him of old!"

"I assure you this is not so," he replied, with gentle slowness. "I think very highly of certain qualities which you possess, and I even find great charm in your society; but I must own that in the matter of the intellect, I cannot help observing that heaven has gifted men in a manner which has been denied to your sex. What woman has ever brought to perfection any serious work? Come, let us see—let us compare. It is only by comparing that one can arrive at the truth. Let us see: what woman has ever written a great poem —a *Faust*, for instance?"

The only woman's poem important in form that I ever read was *Aurora Leigh;* but I was sure that if any one at table knew it, it would be only Monsieur Berthier, and that he would of course immediately launch either Milton or Shakspeare at my head, so I held my tongue.

"At all events there is one great woman writer at the present moment in France," said Monsieur Dessaix; "what do you say to Georges Sand? She may not be a writer of poems, but a great poet she undoubtedly is, although her works are in prose."

As he spoke, I saw—did I see?—yes—with my own eyes—I saw him stick his fork into a little piece of fried bread which was upon Miss Hamilton's plate, and transfer it to his own; there were several bits, and one by one he took them all. She only laughed, and abused him playfully. I looked anxiously towards Madame Olympe— she coloured deeply and appeared greatly shocked and displeased.

"Nevertheless I hold by my position," said Monsieur Berthier, with insistive mildness. "What woman has written, or ever will write, a *Faust*—a *Hamlet?* What woman has ever painted a fine picture? What woman has ever composed a great opera? Even as executants they are surpassed by men."

"I deny it," said Ursula, vehemently. "If you have had your Talma and your Rubini, we have had our Siddons and our Pasta, and our Malibran, and we still have our Pauline Viardot!"

"Even in pianoforte playing," continued Monsieur Berthier, smiling, "what woman ever played like Liszt for instance?"

"Oh!" cried Miss Hamilton, "if it is to be a question of physical strength, of course I give in!"

"Not at all—not at all," persisted Monsieur Berthier; "but what woman ever approached on the piano the delicacy and the sentiment of Chopin's playing?"

"Ah, who indeed!" said Monsieur Dessaix, who had known and loved him. "What was it like? When one seeks a similitude for it, one thinks involuntarily of things delicious and evanescent in nature—the shadow of the flight of a bird —the tremulous flicker of leaves over a bit of sunny ground—and so human too! it was the very embodiment of rêverie: nothing was ever in the least like it!"

"You see," said Monsieur Berthier, laughing gently, "that even in things which only require tenderness and delicacy, in which one would naturally imagine that the superiority would lie with your sex——"

"And so it does!" cried Ursula. "You are below your subject,—or you would be aware that the two functions which most nearly affect the happiness of the human race, are confided solely to the sensitive epiderme and the unequalled delicacy of touch of women—the rolling of your tobacco and your tea-leaves!"

The dinner wound up with an ugly ceremony enough: they all rinsed their mouths and gargled their throats, and spat into their finger-glasses, with as much energy as if they had been cleaning their teeth in their own bedrooms. Lady Blankeney and her daughter alone, like women of principle, only just wet the tips of their fingers, after the English fashion. Miss Hamilton was much more like a foreigner than an Englishwoman in all her ways; as for me, I have no strength of mind, and so, though I thought it rather nasty, I did as Rome did; after which we returned to the drawing-room, in the same order in which we had left it.

"Well, my dear Countess," said Lady Blankeney, blandly smiling, "and what do you think of our two geniuses?"

"Geniuses!" said Madame Olympe, looking like thunder. "I don't know what their morals may be, but I never saw such bad manners in all my days;"

I glanced round in great anxiety, for Madame Olympe's indignation had hardly confined itself to a whisper: most fortunately both Ursula and Monsieur Dessaix had left the room.

"O dear! no, really! I *am* so grieved!" said Lady Blankeney in a nervous flutter. "I know our dear Ursula *is* rather peculiar. I always think geniuses *are* a little peculiar; but, dear me, I *am* so sorry! But was there anything very—very—eh?"

"I never beheld such ill-bred familiarity in all my life!" said Madame Olympe.

"He calls her thou—four, five, six," said Miss Maria, who had taken some tapestry-work out of a bag and was counting her stitches.

"He ate out of her plate," cried Madame Olympe. "It is disgusting!"

"Thirteen, fourteen, fifteen — she took his bread," said Miss Maria, with a spiteful smile.

"Pray has this sort of thing been going on all the time?" asked Madame Olympe, turning severely upon Lady Blankeney.

"O dear, no!" stuttered Lady Blankeney, scared to death. "No—I rather think not—I should not exactly say so."

"He kissed her when he came—twenty-four," said Maria.

"Kissed her!" shouted Madame Olympe.

"Oh, good gracious me, Maria!" exclaimed poor Lady Blankeney. "Why, never! I *really* think there *must* be some little mistake here!"

"Twenty-eight—I saw him do it," said Maria, with a quiet giggle.

While I was lying on the sofa, listening with regret to the storm of opinion that was setting in against Miss Hamilton—for whom, in spite of her strange ways, I could not help feeling the strongest attraction—I heard her and Monsieur Dessaix tranquilly pacing up and down together before the house. Suddenly Jeanne, who was at the window, shut it down very quickly and softly, and coming up to me said, in a low voice :—" My heavens, she is smoking! We must prevent Maman from looking out."

"Dearest Madame Olympe," I said—arresting her progress just as by some odd instinct she was crossing the room and making straight for the window—"would it be too much to ask you for the little cushion which is lying in the chair close by you?" She brought it, and arranged it tenderly under my head. I then took her hand, holding it fast while I spoke to her, until in a fit of absence she quite forgot her original purpose, and subsided gradually into a seat beside me, where I kept her talking about mother, until at last the danger was over and I saw Ursula and her friend reappear.

The beginning of the evening did not go off comfortably. None of the component parts of our little society seemed to amalgamate; they all fell asunder in a helpless, hopeless sort of way. Monsieur Charles went fast asleep in one of the large arm-chairs. Miss Maria worked on, never opening her lips except to count her stitches. Monsieur Kiowski and Monsieur Berthier were at the other end of the room, looking over some valuable prints. Monsieur Jacques made an attempt to speak to Lady Blankeney, but she withdrew from him with an extremely offended air, and went and sat by the chimney, where she dribbled away in never-ending inanity about Lady This, and Sir Somebody Something, to Madame Olympe, who was standing before the fire with her gown well tucked up in front, rocking herself backwards and forwards in displeased abstraction. Both Ursula and Monsieur Jacques seemed rather isolated and neglected. I do not know whether she perceived it, but he certainly did. Presently she came and placed herself at the table which stood before my sofa.

"Are you obliged always to lie down?" said she. "Can you occupy yourself in that position? Do you ever play at games? Will you play a game of chess with me?"

The chess-board was on the table before us, so we opened it, and began a game. After we had been playing some time, Monsieur Dessaix, having no one to speak to, came and sat down by us.

"Ursula," said he, in a low voice, "dost thou

think I have made an agreeable impression upon thy friends?"

"I daresay you have. Why shouldn't you?" she answered. "It is your move, Miss Hope."

"Thou art mistaken, my darling. They detest me—thy new friends I mean: thy great countess who warms herself so majestically at the fire there; Lady Blankeney, too, has begun to hate me."

"Check!" said I.

"Thou art brimful of fancies," said Miss Hamilton. "Why on earth should she hate thee?"

"Didst thou not see how she moved to the other side of the room just now?" he replied. "That was to avoid me."

I, who had seen her do it, and heard the conversation which had preceded this performance of hers, knew very well that it was no fancy of his, but that she had simply gone over to the enemy and made up her mind to repudiate him from the moment that she discovered that he was not a success.

"Dost thou mean to sing to-night?" he continued, in his usual little level tone of discontent.

"Do not do it; it always has a much better air to refusé the first evening."

"Check!" said I again. "No, you can't move there—that is in check to the knight."

"Dost thou believe that they will ask me to play? It would be indecent of them to do it after my journey—wouldn't it? I shall refuse; they are so insolent, these aristocrats? Thou dost not know them as I know them," said Monsieur Jacques.

"There, Jacques! you have made me lose my castle!" cried Miss Hamilton.

"I will be silent, since I bore thee," he said, and he took up a book and pretended to read. Presently, however, he looked at her over the top of it very mournfully, and began again :—

"My Ursula! Is it possible that I bore thee!"

"Check," said I. "No, you cannot go there on account of the white bishop."

"That I bore thee!" he ejaculated, with his melancholy little dark eyes fixed upon her.

"Oh, Jacques, *do* hold your tongue!"

"I'm afraid it's checkmate," said I.

"And that's your fault!" she cried, laughing, and gave him a box on the ear.

I looked round in an agony. Luckily no one was turned our way, and nobody saw it, except little Jeanne, who was sitting by my side; she screwed up her mouth very tight, and opened her eyes very wide, but I knew she was safe, and would tell no tales.

"Mademoiselle Ursula, are you too tired to sing at all this evening?" said Monsieur Berthier. "It is some years since I have had the pleasure of hearing you, but I have not forgotten those beautiful chest notes; you have, no doubt, made great progress since that time. You were only just beginning to learn then, you know."

"Do not sing, I entreat of thee," murmured Monsieur Jacques in her ear; "it is better *genre* not to sing the night that one arrives."

"Oh, do not prevent her from doing what would make us all so happy," said I; "that is," turning to her, "if you really are not too tired."

"No, indeed," she replied. "I should like to sing to you, if Madame de Caradec does not object to our using the piano."

Madame Olympe rose from her seat sullenly, without a word, and went and opened the instrument; after which she proceeded to light two small lamps. Monsieur Kiowski was anxious to be of use to her, and fidgeted round her with a lucifer-match, which he had rushed to get from the hall; but she ignored him completely; steadily, in the face of his match, lit her lamps at a private bit of paper of her own, which was an hour taking fire, and nearly walked over him as she stalked up to the piano and placed them upon the desk.

Ursula then sat down and sang the famous air of "Lascia ch'io pianga" with such breadth and pathos, and such a glorious contralto voice, that we were all thrown into a state of the greatest commotion—all except Miss Blankeney. I looked at her, and I could see her lips forming Four, five, six to herself. "Brava! brava! e mille volte brava! mi consolo tanto!" shouted Monsieur Kiowski, who had drawn an arm-chair exactly opposite to her when she began, into which he had thrown himself rather protectingly and with the air of a connoisseur, and who now jumped up from it with all the real enthusiasm of an artist. As for me, my nerves were in a very shaky condition, and I had never heard anything half so beautiful, and I began to cry. She was going to get up, when Madame Olympe, who was standing behind her, put her hands upon her shoulders, and saying with emotion, "Oh! how *grand* it is! Some more, some more!" pressed her down into her seat. She sang for us until she was quite tired —whatever she knew by heart, for her music had not yet been unpacked, and as soon as she had done one thing there was a cry for another. At last Madame Olympe took her hands, and saying in a penetrating voice, "Oh! *how* you sing! how happy you are to be able to give such *deep* happiness to others!" embraced her. "And your friend Monsieur Dessaix," she continued, turning to him courteously—for the music had melted away all her wrath—"he plays the violin I believe? Will he not play us something?"

"Madame la Comtesse," he said, getting upon his feet, and assuming an air of sickly solemnity, which was nearly the death of Jeanne, "I trust that you will deign to dispense with my compliance this evening. My health is delicate—I suffer incredibly from my nerves—genius must wear its crown of thorns." Here he smiled with idiotic fatuity, and danced about upon his legs. "Tomorrow, yes, to-morrow, I shall be most happy!" and then he clicked his heels together and bowed, quite convinced that he had done the thing in the most perfect manner imaginable. Madame Olympe returned to Miss Hamilton, and putting her arm kindly round her said,—

"But some one else must do something. She must have some rest, or we shall kill her!"

"Oh, I will play," said I; and I went and played some of Heller and Schumann's smaller pieces. We then made Monsieur Kiowski sing. This was not easy of achievement. First of all he said that he really never sang at all; then that he was shockingly out of practice, then that he knew nothing by heart, then that he had a bad cold, and had completely lost his voice; after which he was made to confess that he had brought his music with him, and was despatched upstairs to fetch it. I undertook to try and accompany him, and he sang several of Gordigiani's songs quite charmingly, with a sweet little impertinent tenor voice, great sentiment, and the most perfect Italian accent. These Florentine airs led to a comparison between the Tuscan and Neapolitan melodies, and then Ursula sat down again to the piano, and gave a number of examples of the latter with infinite fun and spirit. Our

F

evening had become brilliant under the influence of her brilliant gift; and all the clouds were swept clean away from Madame Olympe's noble face, which was radiant with pleasure.

At last Miss Hamilton got up, and we went together to the table where Monsieur Jacques was sitting building card-houses in solitary grandeur.

"Thou hast sung like an angel," he said, "but thou singest too much. One day thou wilt die with thy mouth open. Why did nobody ask me to play? I suppose they did not wish to hear me; but it would have been more civil at any rate, I think, to ask me."

"But, my dear Jacques, you *were* asked," answered Miss Hamilton, "and you refused. I heard you with my own ears refuse. Why, before there was any question at all of music, you declared your positive intention of not playing."

"Certainly I did," he said; "nothing should have induced me to play; but still if they had wished very much to hear me, they could have asked me a second time. It might have been very bad, but it might have been very good,—how could they tell? Thou thinkest that I am vain, and feeble, and peevish? Ah, how well thou knowest me! Thou, who art so strong, must often despise me at the bottom of thy heart? Confess that thou dost! Thou needest say nothing! I see it in thy nose. What a nose thou hast, my Ursula! It is always going, going, going; it is like a rabbit's. Why didst thou sing nothing of mine this evening? Dost thou not like my music? Dost thou not believe in my talent any more?"

"The accompaniments of thy songs are too difficult," said Ursula, "and I do not know them by heart."

"I know them by heart," said Monsieur Jacques, "and I could have played them if I had been asked."

Luckily, Lady Blankeney and Madame Olympe rose at this moment, and an end was put to his complaints.

Nothing could be more amiable and pretty than Miss Hamilton's manner when she found that we were to share the same room. "And I will call you Bessie and you must call me Ursula for ever afterwards," she said, as she kissed me and wished me good-night.

We had been in bed about an hour when I was awakened by the noise of a knocking at the wall against which Miss Hamilton's bed was placed; and, presently, Monsieur Dessaix's voice came through the thin partition quite distinctly.

"Ursula, art thou asleep?" it said, in a low tone.

"Yes, I am," she answered, sitting bolt upright in her bed. "What dost thou want?"

"Oh, Ursula!" moaned the voice from the next room, "thou sleepest, but I cannot close my eyes!"

"Why, what's the matter? what's amiss?"

"Dearest Ursula," it went wailing on, "there is a dreadful smell in my room. Oh, it is such a smell! That is why I cannot sleep. Good-night, my angel!"

"Good-night, my good Jacques," she answered gently.

I heard her lie down, and we were both nearly asleep again—at least I certainly was,—when the tapping recommenced at the head of Ursula's bed, and woke me once more.

"Oh, my Ursula! Dost thou sleep?"

To Bed, but not to Sleep.

She started up in bed. "Oh, what is it, Jacques? Do for heaven's sake try to rest!"

"My darling," said the mournful creature from the other side, "I can't think what it can be. . . . Oh, Ursula, it is such a smell! I do so wish thou couldst smell it! . . . . Good-night, my angel!"

"Good-night — good-night," she answered. "Be quiet and try to forget it."

We once more closed our eyes, but we might have spared ourselves the trouble, for in about ten minutes a series of hurried and exultant thumps were executed upon the partition.

"Dearest!" his little cracked voice uttered in jubilant accents, "I have found them! . . . . They are apples! . . . . They are in a little cupboard under my bed! . . . . Good-night, my Ursula! good-night!"

The stable clock struck one as he spoke, and after that he allowed us to repose in peace.

PART II.

THE next morning Ursula and I had a long talk together about Monsieur Jacques. She told me that she had known him ever since she was sixteen years old, and that he was established in Florence when she and her father were living there; and then she said, in a sort of natural way which went to my heart,—

"He had nobody, and I had nobody, and so we drew together."

"But Colonel Hamilton was with you then, wasn't he?" said I.

"Oh, yes," she answered; "but papa never cared at all about the things I cared for, and then I usedn't to see much of him—I never was much with him—but I loved him dearly for all that,"— and her eyes filled with tears. "At first I was too young to go into the world, and then Jacques used often to come and spend the evening with me because it was so lonely when papa was away dining out or at the theatre."

"And used you to be left quite entirely alone?" said I. "Had you no woman in the house to look after you?"

"Oh, I had the Meneghina, our old Italian maid," she replied. "She generally used to bring in her work and sit with us. When I was eighteen, I thought that, perhaps, papa would then take me out with him, but I think he liked best going out by himself; it left him so much more free and independent. I suppose that was the reason why he never introduced me to any of his friends, or took me to the houses of the people that he knew."

"Then did you never go out at all?" said I.

"Oh, yes, I went out a little, but into quite a different set from papa's. I went to Giambattista's parties—Giambattista Giacomelli was my singing-master. Such a dear old fellow! and he had delightful musical parties every Sunday, to which papa allowed me to go,"

"Well," said I, "but did you go to these parties alone?"

"No," she answered. "Our landlady, the

Del Nero, went to them, and I went with her. She lived in the floor above us, and I used often to go up there of an evening when papa went out and they were at home. It was there that I first met Jacques. The Del Nero used to play splendidly on the piano, and he used to accompany her on the violin. She, too, had musical evenings which were charming; the society was entirely Italian, composed of doctors, lawyers, artists and literary men—all clever and well educated. This is the only really well-educated society in Florence; the fashionable people are of an unbelievable ignorance. The Del Nero's husband was an avvocato. I don't think I saw any English faces, except those of papa and one or two of his men friends, in all the years that I lived in Florence. I was fourteen when I went there, and I am twenty-four now; that makes ten whole years, doesn't it?"

Her account of her life sounded very strange and desolate. Her father seemed to have taken such little care of her, that I felt really shy of asking her many questions. Later, the outline was filled up for me by Monsieur Jacques, who told me that Colonel Hamilton was a perfect monster of selfishness—altogether the most heartless man that he had ever met with. Instead of taking the least pleasure or interest in his child, he was, on the contrary, in despair at having a daughter of that age, and kept her entirely in the background. He used to go about in all the bad fashionable society of Florence, got up in the most youthful style and lavishing every luxury upon himself, while poor Ursula had hardly decent clothes to her back. More than once the good Del Nero had given her a gown, without which she would have been unable to accompany her even into the modest Italian circle to which they belonged; and in spite of all this, Monsieur Jacques told me that she had perfectly doted upon her father while he lived, and had nearly died of his death. It seems that he had retained his handsome looks and charm of manner to the last, and although he was as hard as a stone, always contrived to be good-tempered and pleasant at home.

Certainly nothing could be much more strange than the state of things between Ursula and her friend. At first I supposed it must be foreign;—it was, however, evidently not so much foreign as individual, for it excited far greater indignation in

Madame Olympe's mind than it did in mine. I had certainly never seen any manners in the slightest degree resembling theirs; but after the movement of surprise which they created in me at first, I soon got accustomed to them, and the whole relation had a side so touching and pretty, that, notwithstanding its somewhat unusual manifestations, I began by accepting, and ended by sympathizing with it. Ursula's strength and decision were like health to the little morbid mortal who looked up to her as morally far superior to himself, and his devotion and knowledge of the world were everything to so young a woman, whose impulsiveness, combined with her extreme simplicity of character, tended to put her greatly in the power of designing people. In spite of the weakness of his nature, the singleness of his desire after her welfare invested him in some sort with the authority of a father or a brother.

The change of air and of surroundings had already done me so much good, that on the Wednesday morning I was actually able to take a little walk with Margery before breakfast. The park is not very large, but there are charming walks all round it: not shrubbery, but regular woodland paths; it being, in point of fact, simply a bit of the forest enclosed. The weather was quite heavenly, and the purity and elasticity of the air something enchanting; one felt all the time as if one were drinking vivifying draughts of some electric water. The soil is sandy, drying directly after the heaviest rain, and the air is of the light, exhilarating quality which always goes with that particular kind of soil. Poor Margery asked me anxiously when I meant to go home, and was greatly relieved when she found that I did not mean to exceed the limit I had originally fixed to my visit. She was comfortable enough, she said, but they were an unsociable set, and did not live in the least like English servants. At about eight in the morning every one went down, took a little bowl from a shelf on the wall, got it filled with *café au lait*, and drank it with a little bit of bread-and-butter, standing. There was nothing like a breakfast table, and nobody thought of sitting down. They then all dispersed, and did not meet again until after our *déjeûner à la fourchette* at about twelve, when they had their second breakfast. This was devoured in all haste, after which they again separated. There was nothing like a servants'-hall, as in our great houses, and no assembling in the kitchen as in our small ones. The men-servants remained by themselves, and the women sat entirely in their own rooms. Excellent rooms they were, Margery told me; large, airy, with every comfort, and a look of prettiness and elegance that was quite unknown with us. Supper, which took place after our late dinner, brought them together again, but only for the purpose of eating—which ceremony, like the previous one, was got over as speedily as possible.

At breakfast we had Monsieur le Curé, from Marny—a stalwart, weather-beaten-looking man, with a demure, rather sly, but not bad countenance. He sat between Madame Olympe and myself, and was putting her *au courant* of the affairs of the village. They did not appear to be in a very flourishing condition, as far as morality was concerned, for he continually began accounts of proceedings which, after the three first suggestive words, had to be imparted in a whisper, to the great annoyance of poor Madame Olympe, who nevertheless could not help laughing at the absurdity of the thing. The curé would begin:—
" Madame la Comtesse has doubtless heard about

Thérèse Pichon? Is she aware that only three nights ago . . . . ?" and then a long whisper. I endeavoured immediately to begin a little subject with Monsieur Kiowski; but I saw, by his absence of all rejoinder, and the frightful vacancy of the eye he riveted upon me, that he was straining every nerve to catch the luckless Thérèse's little adventure. A minute afterwards it would be, with great gravity, "Has Madame la Comtesse been told that Auguste Leroy is going to leave the village? It appears that on Wednesday last, one of the keepers going his rounds in the forest at midnight, found him. . . ." Then another whisper, and at the end, " His brother says that after that he will keep him no more. *Dame!* It is the third time that it happens!" At last there came a story, in which "la Malheureuse" played a great part, and was repeated with strong reprobatory emphasis. This story was a very long one, and presently reached such an appalling crisis that even poor Madame Olympe, who was, as one may say, "to the manner born," could stand it no longer, but calling out, "The boat! the boat!" hastily jumped up from table, and ran to the window.

"The boat! where's the boat! let me see the boat!" cried Monsieur Kiowski, throwing himself impetuously into the spirit of the thing, and nearly overturning the table in the wild excitement with which he tore to the window. It was only the boat which comes down the river every morning regularly. To-day it appeared in the very nick of time, and deserved extra notice: but I observed that whenever it appeared it always created a slight agitation. I suppose that the general monotony of their lives ended with making little events become important in their eyes. When it had passed out of sight they returned to the table.

I do not think that in the whole course of my life I ever beheld any human creature devour as Monsieur le Curé did: he ate largely of soup, of both the hot dishes and of the three cold ones, besides the salad and other vegetables—which, although always handed round separately (and not, as we do in England, taken as an accompaniment to the meat), appeared to be thrown in as it were, and quite to go for nothing. He then, in addition to his wine-and-water, had a tremendous jorum of *café au lait*, and topped it all up with two gigantic tumblers of ale, and the fatal pastry-cake and honey that I have before alluded to. His face, always scarlet, had become gradually purple under this trying process, and I expected every moment that he would have some dreadful seizure or other. Madame Olympe told me that it was almost as if he laid in his week's provision of good substantial food, when he came up to breakfast at the château; that he was miserably poor, and a most excellent creature, half-starving himself in order to be able to give, out of his wretched pittance, some assistance to his still needier neighbours. The curé is an entirely different being from our country clergyman : very hardworking and exemplary, but in quite a different way, and altogether simpler and more homely. It is not at all an uncommon thing abroad to see the curé thinking nothing whatever of assisting in manual labour, but working in the field with his neighbours, and helping them to get in their hay. In one respect, a good sense is shown in Catholic countries, which might be imitated in the Church of England with infinite advantage : their clergymen are by no means necessarily preachers. The functions are divided : he who has the gift of an eloquent tongue, speaks to the souls of his parishioners through their ears, and he who has it not, labours in the vineyard of the Lord silently.

Madame Olympe was much troubled this morning about her poor housekeeper, who during the night had become a great deal worse. The illness had assumed a very grave character, and before breakfast she had been removed to the village, and put under the care of the good Sœur Marie and of a regular nurse. Monsieur le Curé had brought satisfactory news of her safe arrival at Marny, and told us that on the whole she had borne her little journey fairly well.

After breakfast Monsieur Kiowski brought down his portfolios, and we passed a delightful two hours looking over his drawings, and some beautiful photographs which he had brought from Italy. Nothing was ever more kind and amiable than he was: bringing them all to the sofa for me, and improvising a sort of desk with the pillow, so that I could see them without tiring either my head or my hands. "That is St. Peter's," said he, a little unnecessarily; "the largest and most important church of Rome. It is in St Peter's that all the ceremonies of the Holy Week take place, and from it that the world-famous benediction is given. That is the Colosseum; formerly it was the arena in which the combats of the gladiators were witnessed; now it serves the purpose of a church, where people come to hear preaching, and to pray at little stations which have been erected in it."

I was amazed at the delicacy and beauty of his drawings; Monsieur Berthier, too, was charmed with them. "The fineness of touch is quite incredible!" he said several times with enthusiasm, and indeed in some of the drawings it was really impossible to see where the strokes were by which the enchanting result was arrived at. Mothers and children seemed to be favourite subjects with him: his book was filled with children in every sort of position: his babies are perfect,—so unconscious, and all the little lovely melting bits—the round of the temple and cheek, the little soft way in which the head sits on the neck of a baby—felt with a maternal tenderness that seemed quite extraordinary in a young man. Presently I came, among the drawings, upon a lovely sketch of the river and forest taken from the château. I exclaimed when I recognized it, and in the kindest and most charming way he immediately entreated me to accept it. I felt dreadfully ashamed at having so valuable a present made me, but it was so pretty and so delightful a souvenir of my visit, that I could not bring myself to refuse it; and all the less that I saw by his manner that it would be a real pleasure to him to give it to me. Ursula Hamilton was in ecstasies over all the drawings, but most especially about a coloured sketch of the picture Monsieur Kiowski was now engaged upon. The subject was the death of Titian: it was wonderfully harmonious and full of character. There was one head—that of a pupil of Titian's—a soft, young, dark Italian face, that was full of sentiment; and there were two women—one in pale crocus-coloured draperies, with a tiger-lily in her hand, and another in a sort of gold and brown brocade, with her back turned and her head thrown over her shoulder—that were quite magnificent.

"How I do wish I could paint!" said Ursula.

"Why don't you?" said Monsieur Kiowski. "If I were not going to-night I would teach you. With Miss Hamilton's feeling for art, she would soon learn—wouldn't she, Monsieur Berthier?"

"In water-colours," said Monsieur Berthier.

"Why not in oils?" asked Ursula impetuously "Ah, I see!" she added: "*la femme—la femme—et toujours la femme!*" and she came and sat down impatiently by my sofa. "I do get so sick of the way he always goes maundering on about the inferiority of women! I am sure you don't agree with him—you don't believe him, do you?"

"I think we are different creatures," said I, "but I do not see that difference necessarily implies inferiority: as we are inferior to them in certain faculties of the mind which they possess"——

"Yes," she interrupted, "the heavy, slow, tiresome ones——"

"So," continued I, laughing, "I also think that they are inferior to us in other mental qualities which belong entirely, or, at all events, in a much higher degree of perfection, to us. Moreover, I believe that these very differences were beneficently bestowed upon us, 'not to doubtful disputations,' but that man might strengthen the spirit of woman in the bearing of her burdens, and that woman might lighten the heart of man in the carrying of his—that each might be, in their very unlikeness, a comfort, a joy, and a completion to the other."

"At all events you are fair," said Ursula. "You meet one half way, but I felt inclined to hurl things at him yesterday at dinner when he went pottering on with his *Faust* and his *Hamlet*, and his *Hamlet* and his *Faust*. Who ever said that metaphysics, abstract speculation (the least useful of all things, by the way,) were the forte of women? But it is a perfectly different matter with the passions—they belong to us every bit as much as to men, and I don't see why we shouldn't be able to delineate them quite as well. It's all very well to talk,—but what sort of intellectual nourishment do women get? What is called their education consists for the most part of nothing but a series of abridgments, filtered through miserable smatterers. Let a woman just for once have the mental training that almost every man gets, and then we shall see—"

"Whether she will write a *Hamlet?*" said I, smiling.

"Well, perhaps she may not be able to write a *Hamlet*, but I can't for the life of me see why she shouldn't write an *As You Like It*."

"*As You Like It!*" I echoed in utter amazement.

"Yes—*As You Like It*—why not? That is not powerful: it is not even passionate. Don't you see that I am taking up a modest position?"

I couldn't help it; I burst into a peal of laughter from which I was only roused by the tears of mortification which I saw standing in her eyes.

"My dear child," said I, "calmness is power, and the strongest spirits are not those who awaken tumult in our breasts, but those who bring us into peace. As for *As You Like It*, I love that play so dearly, that I believe on the whole I would rather have written it than any of the others. It seems to me to have a divine quality about it: it leaves one as a fine landscape does—with eyes dimmed by mists of tenderness, not of sorrow, and with a heart adoring God and gentler towards one's kind."

Meanwhile Lady Blankeney and Maria had got one of Monsieur Kiowski's sketch-books in their hands the wrong way upwards, and were, apparently with the greatest interest, inspecting the slight pencil landscapes upside down. At last, after having gone through it scrupulously from beginning to end, they put it upon the table.

"Did you like them?" asked Ursula, drily, when they had done.

"Quite charming!" said Lady Blankeney, smiling. "Such a treat. By-the-way, my dear Ursula," she continued, "I have heard from the Marquise de Verneuil this morning, a most civil kind note (nothing like the Faubourg St. Germain after all, is there?), and she is quite in despair at your not coming; but I hope you will revoke that cruel decision."

"I think your decision was the cruel one," answered Ursula. "I have a friend come from another country to see me; I beg you to get Madame de Verneuil's permission that he should accompany us, and you entirely decline doing so."

"Why, my dear Ursula," said Lady Blankeney, rather embarrassed, "you are such a dear ardent creature, and the moment an idea runs away with you there is no making you understand. You see it is a very small, select thing."

"If Jacques is not fit company for them," said Ursula, "neither am I."

"But, my dear child, the thing is so simple," said Lady Blankeney.

"Quite so," retorted Ursula; "he is not going, neither am I."

"But, my dear, she's *delighted*," said Lady Blankeney—"quite delighted, on the contrary—so very anxious to make his acquaintance,—I've got the letter here," she said, tapping her pocket, "and she will only be too charmed——"

"Then you thought better of it and wrote after all?" said Ursula. "Was it after you heard Jacques play?"

"Well, I don't exactly remember what day it was," said Lady Blankeney, getting red and hesitating.

"But it was after you heard him play ——," said Ursula. "Pray, is there to be music at Madame de Verneuil's?"

"Yes," said Lady Blankeney; "she gives the best musical parties in Paris, and as I happened in my note to mention your friend's great talent, why then of course in hers she said she would be only too enchanted."

"Oh, and I am going to sing, I suppose?" said Ursula.

"Why, of course," said Lady Blankeney. "We quite reckon on you, my dear. The dear Marquise was in ecstasies when she heard how beautifully Monsieur Dessaix played, and I'm sure she's only too happy to have him. She says so in her note here,"—again tapping her pocket. " Would you like to see her note ?"

"O dear, no. Pray don't trouble yourself, Lady Blankeney," said Ursula. "We shall neither of us go. I do not mean to sing anywhere but in my own home." (Poor Lady Blankeney looked terribly chapfallen.) "And as for Jacques, he is not professional a bit more than myself; he is in no need whatever of money, and therefore I don't exactly see why he should go and play for a woman whose house you considered too good for him until you thought of making use of him."

"Oh, my dear Ursula, you really have such a way of putting things; but I'm sure you couldn't —you wouldn't—it would be *such* a disappointment!" besought poor Lady Blankeney, in utter dismay. "It has all been my fault—I assure you it has all been my fault—my little nervous way, you know. If it hadn't been the Faubourg, it would have been quite, quite different you know ;

but it is always so select there! But now that she has written to say how delighted she is to make your acquaintance—yours and Monsieur Dessaix's—(and so select as she always is!)—I really don't know what you would have. Isn't it quite true, Maria?" she said, appealing to her daughter in her despair.

"Oh, quite true—ten," calmly said Maria, who had got to her work again and had not the smallest idea what her mother was talking about.

"Very well, then," said Ursula. "In that case we will go——"

"Now that is so nice and sweet of you!" interrupted poor Lady Blankeney, with a ray of hope.

"But," continued Miss Hamilton, gravely, "I will not sing, and Jacques shall not play, and that will give your select Marquise all the more time to become acquainted with us."

Lady Blankeney's face fell so dismally that I was sadly afraid she was going to cry. Just then Madame Olympe came up, and proposed an expedition to the Géant—a high hill in the neighbourhood, from which there was a lovely view.

"But what shall I do?" said Lady Blankeney,

dolorously. "I must send an answer to-day. She told me she meant to do without the Trebelli if Ursula went——"

"Then hadn't you better write and tell her to put the Trebelli on again?" said Ursula, coolly.

"Dear me!" said Lady Blankeney, still more dejected. "I don't see how we are to go at all. What is to become of you, Ursula, if Maria and I go?"

"Oh, don't be unhappy about me, my dear Lady Blankeney. Jacques and I shall have a very cosy little evening together at the hotel, I dare say."

"Speak to her, you, my dear Countess! She really doesn't know the things that people will say, and I really am almost beginning to be afraid that—that—she does not care."

"I do not know, and I do not care," said Miss Hamilton, looking at Lady Blankeney placidly.

"When is this party to be?" asked Madame Olympe.

"It's on Saturday next," said Lady Blankeney, "and I must write to-day, and I'm sure I don't know what I am to say after all her kindness about it!"

A little Excursion.

"I'll tell you what," said Madame Olympe. "Write and say that I keep Miss Hamilton here until Monday next—that is if she will stay?" and she turned towards Ursula. An expression of pleasure lit up Ursula's face, which was followed by a slight shade of hesitation.

"Oh, you *and* Monsieur Dessaix I mean, of course," added Madame Olympe, laughing. "And now go and get your things on quickly, all of you; it soon gets cold of an evening now, and it is a longish way that we have to go. Bessy," she continued, addressing me, "go and fetch your hat too. The others will walk, but the pony-chair is ordered for you, and there is a way up, not quite so pretty, perhaps, as the road that they are going, but at least twice as short: I am sure we can manage it with the pony-chair and our steady old horse, and Monsieur Kiowski and I are coming with you."

We had a lovely view, certainly, when we got to the top of the hill; and I think that the intense delight it gave me must have repaid my dear hostess for all her kind thought and hard labour in my behalf; but oh, what that journey up was to my poor rickety nerves, no words can tell.

We went up, and up, and up, through an entirely perpendicular lane, where there existed no road at all. Madame Olympe walked the whole way, pulling the horse up after her by main force, while Monsieur Kiowski pushed behind with all his might. I never was so terrified or so miserable in all my life. Whenever we stopped for an instant in order to allow the poor animal to recover his breath, the carriage rolled back, and frightened me out of my wits. I made one or two feeble propositions about walking, which Madame Olympe peremptorily extinguished. At last, Monsieur Kiowski, seeing that I was on the point of crying, suggested that I was more likely to be made ill by sitting in the carriage and being frightened, than by the fatigue of walking. Upon this Madame Olympe suddenly turned round, and coming close up to me, in a determined way, said, "You are frightened; of what are you frightened? Of being run away with? How is it possible up this steep hill? Of the carriage rolling back? Where can you go to if it does roll back? into the hedge." And she suddenly backed the carriage right into the hedge, to illustrate her words. "There is only one thing that can happen to you, and that is to tumble out; but I do not see what is to make you do that; and if you did, you are but an inch from the ground in this little low chair, and you could not hurt yourself if you were to try."

"Well," said Monsieur Kiowski, who had gone a little way off to take a peep through a break in the trees, "is it decided? Does she get out?"

"Yes," answered Madame Olympe, unhesitatingly. "I have convinced her reason that there is no danger; so she is no longer frightened, and stays in."

After that there was nothing for it but to remain where I was and endure agonies until we reached the summit. That angelic creature Monsieur Kiowski ran ever so far back to possess himself of an enormous stone, very nearly as big as a milestone, with which he toiled up the hill after us, scotching the wheel with it every time that we stopped, and thereby doing away with what had been the most unpleasant of my sensations. At the top we were met by the rest of the party, with the exception of Monsieur Dessaix. He had started with them, it seems, but the moment they began to ascend the hill he had exclaimed to Miss Hamilton, "Ursula, there is danger; I leave thee!" and returned home. I was allowed by Madame Olympe to walk down by the road that I had come, accompanied by Ursula, Monsieur Kiowski, Monsieur Berthier and Jeanne. Lady Blankeney and Maria were driven home the long way by Madame Olympe.

As soon as we reached the château, Lady Blankeney made one final attempt to mollify Miss Hamilton about Madame de Verneuil, but she was entirely inexorable, and so poor Lady Blankeney, with Maria, retreated upstairs, much mortified, to write her letter. I went and established myself upon my sofa, and Madame Olympe made us some tea—after which Ursula began to sing, and then Monsieur Dessaix was prevailed upon to play. He played with Madame Olympe, first, sonatas of Mozart's, as long as the daylight lasted and that they could see; and then he went playing on, compositions of his own: a song of Gretchen, a song of Juliet, a song of Ophelia, a song of Mignon — tender, pathetic, exquisite! and we sat and listened, first into the twilight, then into the dusk, until the last fine passion and the last faint glimmer clung together in an undistinguishable embrace and died into the night. For some seconds after the sound had ceased, we all remained breathless and motionless, bound in a great silent emotion. At last a gentle voice said from out of the darkness, with a little sympathetic sigh, "Ah, how well I did to come back!"

Ursula's hand, which was lying in mine, gave a sudden jump, and Madame Olympe got up, crying, "Why, René, you don't mean that it's you? No—this is too laughable!"

The lamps were lit, and a slight fair man, with chestnut hair and a red beard divided into two points, was presented to me as Monsieur de Saldes. Jeanne was right—*interesting* was the word. Ursula had remained sitting rather behind me, and had not been perceived in the first moments of greeting. At last Monsieur de Saldes caught sight of her, and came forward with an exclamation of pleasure to meet her.

"My dear Ursula, how charmed I am to see you! Forgive my freedom," he added. "When I first knew you, you were no higher than that, you know,"—and he made the measure with his hand in the air.

"Yes, but I have grown since then. I am now as tall as that," she said, drawing herself up to her full height, and drawing her hand up with a lazy charming gesture to a level with her head, "and I am always called Miss Hamilton."

I was amazed at her self-possession; and so, I think, was Monsieur René, for he suddenly flushed and turned with rather an embarrassed manner to speak to Madame Olympe.

"I feel proud of myself," said Ursula to me in English. "I suppose I am the first person who has ever put that man down in his life."

"He does not seem to like it much," said I.

"Good for him!" she answered, with a wicked smile.

"Now tell me what on earth has brought you back to me so soon, René?" said Madame Olympe. "Your erratic proceedings become daily more wonderful."

"Suppose I have come back for the meet to-morrow? Would that be so very wonderful?" said he.

"Yes," said Madame Olympe, "for you knew of the meet before you went, and had no intention whatever of hunting."

"Perhaps I came back to see old friends—who knows?" he said, with a charming smile at Ursula.

"That won't do either," said Madame Olympe. "You forget that I know what took you away in such a hurry. You had better tell the truth at once—it will have to come out at last—come, execute yourself with a good grace, and unfold the mystery."

"If I were to tell you, how you would laugh at me!" he said, laughing himself. "Well, you must know, then, that yesterday evening I thought I would just go for half-an-hour to Madame de Limour's. At this season I made sure of finding her alone, and having a little chat comfortably by her fireside. Not at all. There were at least twenty people—men of science with dowdy wives, literary lions, a German poetess with a goître—and in the midst of all these, such a fish out of water, and more undressed than anything you can conceive, Sophie de Malan! She was in the hands of a hideous man, who, I was told, had just written something about the decomposition of oils. She flew to me at once, held on like grim death, and would not let me go until I had sworn all my great gods that I would dine with her to-day. I really never saw anything so shocking as her appearance. I suppose, like myself, she had expected to find no one, and had put on an old gown—it was a very dirty one—and those naked little high shoulders! I assure you one could see the articulation of her anatomy all down her chest as far as her waist. You never saw such a hideous spectacle in your life!"

"Where was Monsieur de Malan?"

"Oh, she had left him somewhere or other by the seaside in Normandy, and was only herself in Paris for a day or two on business. If he had been there I might have borne it. I always rather liked Malan: but a tête-à-tête with Sophie was more than my poor shattered frame could stand. So I wrote a little note (to be sent at seven o'clock), stating how at the eleventh hour my wretched health obliged me to renounce the promised happiness, &c."

"So that, in point of fact, it is to Madame de Malan's invitation to dinner that we are indebted for the pleasure of seeing you?" said Miss Hamilton.

"Do you know her, Miss Hamilton?" said

Monsieur de Saldes, turning to her. " Oh, though, of course you do! She was at Florence in the old days."

"Yes, she was at Florence in the old days," answered Miss Hamilton, smiling : " but my acquaintance with her was very slight."

" And you are going to England, Olympe tells me," he continued, ." and with Lady Blankeney ? Surely, after the *vita libera* of Italy, England, and under those auspices, will never suit you ? "

" I am afraid the alliance does not seem likely to last very long," said Ursula. "Our points of view upon all subjects are so very different. I don't feel certain how I may like England under my new circumstances. I have come into a fortune, you know; and among other pleasant things have inherited an estate in Devonshire, which I am told is quite lovely. I can fancy liking country-life in England—there is something useful, delightful, and altogether noble about it. Whenever I read or hear about it, it seems to me the ideal life. Each of the two times I have been in England, it has only been to make a hurried visit of a few days to London upon business matters. Oh, how ugly I thought it, and how I hated it! It was almost worth while going there, though, for the joy of returning afterwards to the beloved land. How one's spirits rise the moment one crosses the frontier, and hears people speaking with sweet terminating vowels once more!"

"Yes," said Monsieur Kiowski. "I know nothing like the emotion that the first Italian town gives one after an absence—the well-remembered yet always new aspect of men and things! The faded frescoes on the old palaces—the balconies teeming with crowded flowers; the shops, half in, half out of doors—the barber with the striped curtain drawn back, that the patient may flâner with his eyes while his chin is in jeopardy—the tailor who is always mending a waistcoat on a sort of hob at the entrance of the shop——"

"The limonaro and the water-melon man," interrupted Ursula.

"The ill-shaven priests and slippered women," continued Monsieur Kiowski.

"The groom who has a tenor and the milkman who plays the mandoline!" cried Ursula.

"How noisy—how sunny—how fascinating it all is!" said Monsieur Kiowski.

A Talk about Italy.

"And, sommi Dei! what a stench!" added Monsieur de Saldes.

"I don't mind it!" said Ursula, indignantly.

"You needn't be angry with me for my unromantic climax to your ecstasies," said Monsieur de Saldes. "No one knows better than I do the emotion of a return to Italy. The second time I went to Rome, it was at the end of October, I recollect. I threw open the window of the carriage as we drove from Civita Vecchia: a dense vapour covered all the country, and one could see nothing; but the whole land smelt of the aromatic herbs which the cattle were chewing, and that well-remembered Campagna odour of thyme borne in upon the damp air affected me unspeakably. I lay back in the carriage, and cried like a child: happy tears! why cannot one shed such oftener!"

I felt quite touched. "Humbug!" said Ursula to me in a low voice. It was the first time that she jarred upon me.

"Well," said Madame Olympe. "No one enjoys a trip to Italy more than I do, but I don't think I could live there. I do get so furious with the dishonesty and unreliability of the people—they do cheat and lie so!"

"You must remember," said Ursula, "that going to Italy as you do, and living the hotel life on the great beaten track, you see the very worst specimens of the people. They do not, perhaps, feel the great shame of lying as the English do; but I have known many perfectly dependable Italians, and I think that when they are so at all, they are generally more so than any other people. Quite the most truthful nature I ever met with was an Italian, and that was the Meneghina, our Venetian maid: she was absolutely transparent."

"Yes," said I, "nothing can be more charming than that sort of impulsive candour that you speak of; but at the same time I must say that I like the English notion of the *shame* of a lie. There is something very noble about it, and it belongs altogether to a higher tone of feeling than the involuntary truth-telling which you praise in Italians."

"I have remarked," said Monsieur Berthier mildly, "that the conception of truth among Englishwomen is quite peculiar to themselves; and I must own that it appears to me very often to answer the exact purpose that falsehood does with other people. For example, suppose that an

Englishwoman has happened to go to some place or other, and that she has her own reasons for not wishing it known that she has been there—(such a thing might occur, might it not?)—she comes back, and some one asks her where she has been? She immediately answers, To this place—to that place—to the other place, and thinks that so long as she does not positively deny the having been to the one important spot she is scrupulously truthful. For has she, after all, not indeed been to all these places? More than this, she is even capable of deliberately planning to go to all these places, expressly in order that she may be able with what she regards as perfect truth to enumerate them, and behind them to conceal what she wishes concealed. When I have said what I thought upon the subject—which was that this mode of action appeared to me to be very much like pressing truth into the service of falsehood—I have been received with indignant surprise. The Englishwoman thought she had, on the contrary, evinced a conscientious adherence to truth. Now a Frenchwoman is, for the most part, quite incapable of that sort of thing; if she is in a difficulty she will lie like a trooper, but it will be a direct lie born out of an immediate danger—not that elaborate perversion of the truth in which the Englishwoman permits herself to indulge with so much astuteness and self-complacency."

"The entirely motiveless lies which Roman people often tell, are the most curious of all," said Monsieur Kiowski. "When I was in Rome, I had a most valuable man-servant: he was a man of an education considerably above his station, had been highly recommended to me, and was trustworthy in every way. One day when I came home he announced to me that a gentleman whom he had never seen before had been to call upon me; he had left no name, and he had forgotten in the hall a very curious cane. There was no end to the trouble my poor Giovannino gave himself about this stick. He made inquiries in every direction, and finally had handbills printed and stuck about in the principal shops describing it, and informing the owner where he might recover it. No one claimed it, however, and at last, after many months, considering the matter now quite hopeless, he grew to regard the stick as in a manner his own, and to take it with him when he went out walking. One day more than a year after this circumstance had occurred, he was suddenly stopped in the street by the owner of the cane, who recognized and claimed his property. Giovannino surrendered it joyfully and unhesitatingly, at the same time affirming positively that he had bought it not half an hour ago, and given ten scudi for it. He told me all this himself when he came home—and I, who knew to what trouble and expense the poor fellow's honesty had put him, in vain endeavoured to elicit from him some reason or other for his extraordinary gratuitous falsehood. 'But why, *why* did you say that you had bought it?' I in vain inquired. 'Eh, non saprei!' he only answered with a smile; 'mi è saltato cosi fuori dalla bocca! —it jumped out of my mouth!'"

"After all," said Monsieur de Saldes, "the difference is not merely national, it is also individual in the highest degree. No two English or French people look at truth in the same way: it is a relative thing, and every one sees it from his own point of view. I have a friend whose respect for truth induces him to go about the world hurting everybody's feelings, and making himself perfectly odious; he thinks he is performing a great duty, and is delighted with himself. As for me, I hope I am not more undependable than any one else in serious matters; but I would tell any amount of little insignificant social lies to give a pleasant emotion, and, above all, to spare a moment's pain to any one. *I* think *that* is a duty; he despises me, and I hate him—who is to decide between us? Truth, like everything else, is an entirely relative thing. Did you ever read Renan's *Vie de Jésus*, Miss Hamilton?" he continued. " If you recollect, without wishing in any way to impugn the divine veracity of our Lord, he bids us remember that he was an Oriental, and all but insinuates that his assertions may therefore be taken with a grain of salt. I quite agree with him as far as the question of nationality is concerned; don't you?"

"I hate the blasphemous twaddle of that book," said Miss Hamilton, "and agree with nothing it contains. I think it has been made, in every way, of a great deal more importance than it deserves."

"But it is very prettily written!—have you read it, Miss Hope?" he said, turning to me. "Every one must own that it is prettily written."

"I think," said I, "that the very expression

you make use of, condemns the book. In treating of such subjects, prettinesses are so out of place as to become absolutely shocking to people like myself, of strong prejudices and weak minds."

"Ah, but there are charming pages!" he continued. "And then there is such a perfume of naïveté and of the primitive life in his descriptions of the places! that, too, is original; no one ever did it before."

"Yes," said Ursula, "he has sprinkled the Holy Land with rosewater. It is perfectly of a piece with the idea of presenting the Saviour of the world under the aspect of a garçon d'esprit—'qui a inventé ce genre délicieux des paraboles.' This also, no doubt, has the merit of originality. As you say, nobody ever did it before, and I sincerely hope nobody ever will do it again. Saint Peter denied our Lord, but it was reserved to Monsieur Renan to patronize him."

"Ursula!" called Madame Olympe from the other end of the room, where she was looking out some music, "do tell me what programme I can arrange for the village church on Sunday next? There is going to be a grand confirmation-function, and we want, if possible, to get up something a little more important than usual in the way of music. There is a little woman in the village—the wife of one of our huntsmen—who has a very pretty voice: she and Jeanne can sing a duet together, and we can manage a simple chorus or two; but that will hardly be enough, I am afraid."

"May I sing?" said Ursula. "I should like to sing in a church of all things,—that is, if you don't mind my being a heretic?"

"No, really?" exclaimed Madame Olympe. "Heretic or no heretic, you deserve to go to heaven for such an offer! May you sing? Indeed you shall, since you give me the chance."

"But what shall it be?" said Ursula. "I have only one sacred song in the world—a psalm of Marcello's. It will be the very thing, but it is the only one I possess."

"Well," said Madame Olympe, "that will do for the first song; but you must have two solos—what shall we do for the second? What was that grand air of Stradella's you sang just now?—that was very solemn."

"My dear Madame Olympe," said Ursula, "it is a passionate love-song, and begins with the words, 'Oh del mio dolce ardor, bramato oggetto.'"

"Never mind!" said Madame Olympe. "It is quite magnificent, and you sing it superbly. We must have it. I will look out some Latin words which we will clap upon it, somehow or other. We must have it at any price."

Just then the carriage which was to carry Monsieur Kiowski to the station was announced, and Monsieur Kiowski—who had gone upstairs to get his things together—hurried into the room to bid us good-by.

"Ah," said Madame Olympe, "how splendid this Tantum ergo of Bach's is! We could sing it if we only had a tenor! Jeanne would take the first, Miss Hamilton the second, Charles could sing the bass. It's not at all difficult. Ah, Monsieur Kiowski, why are you going away?"

"I wish I were not," he answered, "and I would sing it for you with pleasure."

"Come back and sing it!" said Jeanne, laughing.

"Very well, so I will!" he said.

"No! will you?" she cried, jumping up, vehemently.

"My dear child," said her mother, "don't you see that he is joking?"

"Not at all," said Monsieur Kiowski; "we will have the Tantum ergo. Your function is for Sunday; I shall be back here on Saturday morning for breakfast and rehearsal."

"It is unheard of," exclaimed Madame Olympe; "but it is too much! Oh, why *do* you go? why *must* you go?"

"It is a pity," answered he, "but I have an engagement that it is important I should keep."

"Well, then, at all events," said Madame Olympe, "you will give us some more days when you come back?"

"Alas, I fear that too will be impossible! On Monday afternoon I have a model coming at two o'clock, and I shall be obliged to leave you on Sunday as soon as I have sung my Tantum ergo. I have been at play so long that I must set to work without delay, or I shall not have my pictures ready for the Academy, and so à revoir, and not adieu! At least that is something," he added, as he kissed her hand. "A revoir, Jeanne! Monsieur Berthier, adieu; you will not be here, I believe, when I return. Miss Hope, we shall meet again on Saturday,—I shall have the pleasure of singing with you on Sunday, Miss Hamilton."

He then turned to Monsieur de Saldes, and with a hasty bow and a "Monsieur j'ai l'honneur de vous saluer!" rushed off. We looked out and saw him drive past the window. We were a little afraid he might be late—suddenly the carriage stops — what can have happened? Monsieur Kiowski leaps out—he tears up the hill by a short path across to the house. Good gracious, he has forgotten something! he will certainly be too late! An instant more—voluble talking in a high key on the steps—in the passage—and he is in the room. "The poor dear Marquis . . . . I never bade him good-by . . . . Pray say a thousand things for me, I entreat . . . . I wouldn't for all the world that he should think himself forgotten!" panting he articulates, and breathless departs. There he goes spinning down the hill again—long grey coat-tails flying in the wind—he's in—off they gallop. Will he catch the train?

"Good gracious, what a whirlwind!" said Monsieur René.

"But what an angel!" said Madame Olympe. "Think of his coming back all that way, and across the sea too, for a single day, to help us with our music!"

"It isn't you, René, who would do that," said Jeanne.

"No," said René, "I should be sorry to do anything so ridiculous. It can be nothing but an intense gratification of the demon of restlessness within him to make a man do such a thing. Of course he could have remained if he had chosen,— but some people like living in a fuss."

"He said he had an engagement," I observed.

"And not with Madame de Malan, or he might have broken it," suggested Ursula.

"Oh, if there is a lady in the case, I say no more," said Monsieur de Saldes. "Only then, of course, the great magnanimity of keeping the engagement rather goes to the ground."

"I know with whom his engagement is," began Monsieur Berthier.

"Oh, who is it?—do tell us!" we all exclaimed in a breath.

"See," said he, looking round at us complacently, "the curiosity of women! Monsieur René is the only person who expresses no desire to become acquainted with Monsieur Kiowski's little secret. You must know, then," he continued, "that Monsieur Kiowski is much interested about a poor sculptor of great merit in Genoa, who has, in spite of his talent, been quite unable to make any sort of way with the public. Last spring, Monsieur Kiowski made him send over one of his best works—a charming little figure of Egeria—with the hope of being able to sell it for him in England. An American gentleman—a Mr. Crittendon Pike—saw the statue at Monsieur Kiowski's studio, and was much struck by it, but came to no decision. Since Monsieur Kiowski has been here, however, he has received a letter from Mr. Pike, stating that he sails for America on Friday, and would like to see the statue again before he goes; and it is for this—for the chance of effecting this sale, that he curtails his holiday, and goes back. I am sure you are all a little disappointed that there is no lady in the matter—are you not? It would have been more romantic? Well, I think it is even prettier so."

"It isn't you, René, who would have done that either," said Madame Olympe, laughing.

"I flatter myself I should not," he answered, warming his feet, and stroking his red beard with a lovely white rose.

Madame Olympe and I then sat down to the

I

piano, and I tried the bass of some duets with her. Suddenly, Monsieur Charles rushed in nearly as impetuously as Monsieur Kiowski. "Olympe!"

No answer but a series of brilliant scales complacently executed with the right hand.

"Olympe! Have you seen Monsieur Kiowski? Did he come back again, Olympe? He will certainly miss his train!"

She went on steadily playing with a darkening visage.

"Olympe! they tell me he came back again? Did you see him? Do you hear me, Olympe? He had then forgotten something? Olympe! had he then forgotten something? He will lose the train!"

When I heard him labouring in vain to be heard, and addressing himself to her with about as much success as if she had been the wall, I unconsciously made a little indication of stopping; but without looking at me she went on pressing my right arm heavily down with her left, with which she at the same time kept on vigorously executing a rummaging bass, and, dashing the forefinger of her right hand into the centre of my page, to show me my place, gave vent to an ominous " Un, deux, trois ! " that sent me floundering back to my duty in a state of abject submission. Jeanne saw the impending storm, and came to the rescue. " What ! " she cried, with the greatest apparent surprise and interest. " Come back, Marquis ? No !—did he really ? He will certainly be too late ! What could it be ! Hyacinthe will know—let us go and inquire." And she carried him cleverly out of the room.

"You are surprised that I did not answer him?" said Madame Olympe. " Of what use would it have been ? Sometimes he goes on calling my name for ten minutes together from the next room, for no other reason than to establish the fact that I am there ! "

How shall I describe the brusque oddity of my dear strange hostess's manner without giving a wrong impression of that warm generous heart ? One of the days that I was there, Monsieur Charles had a slight attack of feverish cold. With what anxious tenderness, with what affectionate devotion, she waited on and served him ! I never saw in any one such strong feelings of compassion. In most people that virtue does not appear to exceed the limits of a sentiment; in her, pity became a passion. Her great beauty and the quiet appreciation which she had of it, without the slightest admixture of coquetry or affectation, was one of the most striking characteristics of this regal and most original of women. I have seen her go across the room and look steadily at her handsome face for minutes together in the glass with a singleness of purpose that nearly made me laugh; but I never saw her squint at herself as she went by, or pretend to arrange something in her head-dress, or adopt any of the little mean expedients that uneasy vanity, male and female alike, resorts to whenever a looking-glass is in question. I have never known but one other handsome woman equally unoccupied with her own beauty. If you had told her to put on her grandmother's nightcap, she would have been quite content to do so, and to look like her grandmother in it. Madame Olympe would have put on the cap, too, in a minute; but somehow her rue would have been worn with a difference, and she would, through an involuntary artistic instinct, have arranged it at once so as to look in it a thousand times handsomer and younger than she did before. Her extraordinary unconsciousness is, I think, perhaps what attracts and attaches one to her more than anything else. She has no more respect-humain than a baby : the sunlight and the shadows flit over her face according to her humours, just as they brighten and darken the face of uncontrolled childhood; and in her and about her there is all the time a sort of grand innocence which makes one laugh, and for which one adores her. She was evidently gradually growing very fond of Ursula and of Monsieur Jacques. The former had got quite to understand her feeling upon the score of manners; and whenever any little passage occurred to bring a gloom over Madame Olympe's countenance, she would break out into a sudden appeal of glorious recitative that ended everything with an embrace. Monsieur Jacques liked Madame de Caradec very much, and had the greatest opinion of her artistic organization ; but he was still frightened to death at her size and her abruptness, and whenever she came into the room used to strike up the air of " See the Conquering Hero Comes," to the great edification of myself and Ursula. Luckily Madame Olympe's acquaintance with Handel was limited. As for me, Monsieur Jacques and I had become sworn friends; he would come to me for a hundred little services, such as numbering the leaves of his music, stitching them together, sewing buttons on his gloves—and he used to call me his providence.

Delightful as they all seemed to consider Monsieur de Saldes, I did not think our party gained from having him—it became less genial at once. One couldn't help a certain feeling of anxiety and responsibility caused by his presence in some sort of undefined way; he was referred to in one's own mind about everything that did, could, or might occur, in a mute, unacknowledged manner, and it threw a coldness over the whole. On the day of his arrival he contrived to escape the natural fate that awaited him in Miss Blankeney, and to take Ursula in to dinner, to Monsieur Jacques' great annoyance, who sat next to me.

"Do not let her marry him," he said to me. "You have obtained such a good influence over her already—exercise it for her profit, I implore you. Do not let her marry him; I am sure he would not make her happy."

"Do you think there is any chance of such a thing?" I asked, in some surprise.

"Things much more improbable have happened," he answered. "He is not good-looking, is he? it is such a worn-out face."

"The eyes are fine," I remarked.

"Mine are fine too," he said, plaintively. "Have you ever looked at them?" and he fixed them on me. "They are like velvet!" he added, with a melancholy air.

I then noticed for the first time how handsome they were. What gave a great peculiarity to his face was that to these very black eyes there was hardly any eyebrow whatever.

"Is it possible that you are jealous?" said I.

"No," he answered, "not precisely. I never desired to marry her myself; and if I were to desire it and that she were to consent, I should certainly cease to desire it immediately; but I have an uncomfortable presentiment about that man—he will love her, or she will love him, and that would make me perfectly miserable."

Lady Blankeney continued very low, poor woman, at her failure about Madame de Verneuil's party, and could not flutter her little frivolous wings at all. Ursula, too, snubbed her upon every possible occasion—rather unnecessarily, I thought. "What shall you do about the Johnsons, Ursula?" said she. "I hear they have arrived in London with letters from Mrs. Egerton for various people, and for you and myself among the number. What shall you do?"

"Do, Lady Blankeney?" said Ursula. "What can you possibly mean?"

"I mean," said Lady Blankeney, "shall you call, or what?"

"If you mean by '*what*,' neglect them, Lady Blankeney, I shall certainly not do that," replied Ursula. "Indeed, I don't see what option I have in the matter. These people come to me recommended by a friend who was extremely kind to me in Italy, so that whoever or whatever they may be I shall do honour to the recommendation, and call upon them as soon as I arrive in London myself, and show them every civility in my power. Don't you intend to go and see them, that you inquire?"

"Well," she said, "I don't quite know yet how that may be. I shall wait a little and see."

"See what?" asked Ursula. "Whether society in general takes any notice of them?"

"Yes," said Lady Blankeney, quite simply.

"I think it will be better just to wait a little and see."

"Who are these people?" asked Madame Olympe. "Is there any reason why they should not be received or visited?"

"O dear, no," replied Lady Blankeney, with the greatest naïveté. "They are very good sort of people indeed; quite so, I believe."

"It's more than a belief, isn't it, Lady Blankeney?" said Ursula. "You know them quite well, don't you?"

"You are personally acquainted with them, then, already, are you?" said Madame Olympe.

"Yes," said Lady Blankeney. "I know them—that is, I did know them once. They were very rich once, and used to give very nice parties indeed, and I used always to go there—always. And now they are very poor, and I never go there now—never."

Lady Blankeney's worldliness was such a good-tempered, impervious, simple-minded sort of thing, that it became really an amusement to me to listen to her, and I could not bring myself to feel indignant and disgusted as Ursula did, whom it never made to smile for a single instant.

We had nearly finished dessert, when Ursula suddenly exclaimed,—

"What in the world are you doing, Jacques?"

He was carefully stroking down both sides of his nose with the first finger of each hand, and then rubbing the points of the fingers together at the end of his nose, as if to rub off some adhesive substance. I had seen him steadily doing this during the last ten minutes.

"That is the way the flies do," he said, looking up at her meditatively. "Hast thou never seen how they clean their bodies, first with their legs going carefully under their wings, and then how they clean their legs by scraping them against each other?" and he did it again. "*Ceci c'est l'éléphant,*" he continued mournfully, and stretching his arm out with a sudden impetuous sort of circular sweep across to Ursula's plate, he picked up from off it a peach which she was just going to eat, and dropped it with a curve from above into his own mouth. The dexterity and the likeness to the creature he was imitating were perfectly marvellous, and perfectly irresistible—even Maria blinked her short-sighted eyes and chuckled faintly. Monsieur René alone maintained a well-bred gravity, and gave the signal for leaving the table by rising at once.

"He detests me," said Jacques, with a sickly smile. "Don't marry him, my Ursula! If thou dost, I shall give thee my benediction" (and he extended two fingers on the top of her head), "and thou wilt never hear of me again."

Ursula laughed and said:—"I should not suit Monsieur de Saldes at all, my good Jacques, and he is far too wise not to be aware of that fact; and as for me, I would a great deal rather marry the man in the moon; so thou hast nothing to fear. *He* hates thee to-night, does he? Last night it was Miss Blankeney. Art thou reconciled to her?"

"No, my angel," he answered, "and never shall be. Thou laughest at all my instincts, but they are perfectly correct. It is an affair of magnetism, all that, and to a magnetic subject like myself first impressions are quite infallible. But besides the warnings of presentiment and instinct which thou treatest with contempt, there is a fatal something else at work between Meess and myself which causes a deadly and invincible enmity in her bosom. Thou dost not know the misfortune that befell me the day after I arrived in Paris. I lost my way in the hotel, and could not find my own door, and went into her room by mistake. Ah! she was abominable! She had a little rat's-tail of hair hanging down behind, and a huge false plait in her hand; and she had false things on before, and false things on behind, and false things on all round; everything was false except her great teeth and her miserable spindles. She screamed, and frisked wildly about the room, foaming at the mouth, and saying, 'Sortez! sortez!' in a state of fury. But I was glued to the ground, paralyzed with horror, and I couldn't move. At last she hurled her plait at me, and I fled. But these are things a woman never forgives. I know all her little secrets, and she knows that I know them; and ever since that day she has always wished that I was dead. I see it in her face very often; I know the expression quite well."

After we had been laughing a little while at this adventure, Ursula, who was extremely fond of chess, and who wished for her revenge after being beaten the night before, proposed that we should have a game; but a very decided stop was put to this suggestion by Madame Olympe who said.—

" Ursula, you shall not play at chess ; it is a horrid game ; it withdraws people completely from the rest of the society, and swallows them up. I will not have you play. As for Bessie,"—and she stooped down and kissed me,—"she is ill, and may play if she pleases." After which grand but somewhat idle concession, she opened the piano, and the evening was spent in most delightful music. Monsieur René was the first Frenchman I had ever known who was really conversant with the works of Mendelssohn, and really appreciated them. Far from appearing taken with Ursula, he seemed to me to have rather an antagonistic feeling towards her than otherwise. He was singularly cold and niggardly in his praise of her singing, expressing admiration only when positively appealed to by Madame Olympe, in her enthusiasm. She had been singing some things of Rossini's, and after a sort of obliged compliment to her perfect execution of them, he inquired if she never indulged in more serious music than that. She then sang the great air from the *Orfeo* quite magnificently. He, however, merely remarked that it had been originally written for a high tenor, and lost immensely by being arranged for a woman's voice.

"I don't care," said Ursula. "Everybody is not so learned as you, Monsieur de Saldes, and there is so very little real contralto music existing, that I am willing to rob on all sides, wherever I can adapt my theft successfully to my means."

"I will write a new oratorio of Samson," said Monsieur Jacques. "And Samson shall be a contralto, and thou shalt sing it—thou who art strong."

"But how wilt thou write it?" said Ursula—"thou who art not strong? One does but what one is. Thou dear old ninny," she went on caressingly, "thou hast a little soul: how wilt thou do great things with it? But thou hast a tender soul, and a fanciful brain, and of grace, tenderness, and fancy thou wilt always be master. Thou canst but what thou art. Write me a cantata of David before he went up to slay the Philistine, in the flower of his shepherd days, and I will sing that for thee."

Monsieur de Saldes then came to me and begged me to play something. I hesitated a little, for I thought it would sound very poor after the singing, but he insisted, adding, " I believe I am very peculiar, but I confess I like instrumental music (even the piano) better than singing."

I played one after the other of the *Lieder ohne Worte* for him. He knew them all, and it was quite delightful to play to so absorbed and enjoying a listener. His manner, too, was quite charming, so gentle, and with something of a pleasant deference about it—a sort of perfume of another day, and which is quite gone out of fashion. Madame Olympe and Jacques then played us some of Beethoven's sonatas for piano and violin, and I retired to my sofa and crochet, where I was followed by Monsieur de Saldes, who very good-naturedly helped me to wind my wool. Once, during the *Adagio* of the wonderful sonata in C minor, I happened to look up at him; he was holding his hands quite still and the worsted wouldn't run: I saw that his thoughts were far away and his eyes quite full of tears.

PART III.

WE breakfasted earlier on Thursday on account of the hunting. When I came into the drawing-room, I found Monsieur René reading the newspaper in the sun.

"You are going with Olympe to the meet this morning, are you not?" he said. I told him that I was.

"No doubt, as a true Englishwoman, you will have a contempt for our sport, and think fox-hunting infinitely superior; but I am sure that the artistic feeling of which you are so full, will be delighted with the forest. At all events we can lay claim to one superiority in the fact of our hunting being compatible with lovely scenery. Do you ever hunt in England, Miss Hope?"

I told him that in the first place my means did not allow of it, and that in the second I was afraid my nerves would not either.

"I often wish I were less cowardly," said I.

"Ah, do not wish you were other than you are! If women could only be made to comprehend their true position——"

"It will be hard," answered I, laughing, "if between you and Monsieur Berthier we do not get to understand it at last."

"Do not misjudge me," said he. "No one can think more highly of women than I do. In tact, in quickness of perception, in delicacy of feeling, in the unerring justice with which you instinctively arrive at conclusions which we only reach through circuitous paths of cumbrous logic, you stand alone. Steadfastness, patience, tenderness, pity, these are the jewels of your crown— that crown which the strong-minded woman despises in her ambitious endeavour to attain to the male virtues that in her become simply detestable. Yesterday I was so struck with the contrast between yourself and Miss Hamilton when we were speaking of Renan."

"Oh!" answered I, "I liked what she said so much; it was exactly what I was longing to say."

"But, thank heaven, did not," he interrupted.

"Nothing could be a better example of what I mean. The clear, unerring mind was there, the quick perception, the fine moral sense which instinctively detects a want of truth in the heart of things—all that was absent was the male energy of Miss Hamilton; an absence in which, to me, lay the very secret of the charm."

"She is so absolutely truthful and fearless," said I.

"Yes," he answered. "One may admire her, but what one loves is a tender, trembling little woman, doubting of herself, and looking up to man as to her natural guide and protector. Don't you see not only how well this attitude becomes you, but also how admirably it works? When you are womanly you make us manly: these touching and gentle appeals stir all the depths of our buried tenderness, and bring it to the surface. A woman who has no need of this, but can do battle for herself, is generally left to do it. You will see that Miss Hamilton's conquests will not be among men, but among women. Olympe, Jeanne, yourself, already are all more or less at her feet, and this by a natural law. It is simply the masculine element in her, which you are all unconsciously adoring. Now to me, by the same law, she is in consequence of it repellent and unattractive."

" But all men do not feel as you do," said I. " Monsieur Dessaix is devoted to her and he is a man."

" Is he?" said Monsieur de Saldes. " Sometimes I feel quite bewildered between them, and in doubt whether to call her Monsieur Hamilton, or him Mademoiselle Dessaix."

We breakfasted in a great hurry, for Lady Blankeney and Maria were going off by train to Paris. The former took leave of every one but Miss Hamilton and myself with effusion. There was a slight degree of nervous coldness in the manner in which she bade Ursula good-by and said they should meet shortly in Paris, and a charming mixture of condescension and incivility in her farewell to me. I was delighted when they drove off: a little of the mother went a long way, and as for Maria, I do not think I ever beheld any human being so wrapped up in, encompassed by, and utterly saturated with self: the positiveness of the preoccupation became monstrous when contrasted with the negativeness of her nature in every other respect: even the natural laws seemed in her mind to exist as but with reference to herself, and she never spoke of the weather as other people do, remarking in a general way, " It is warm—it is windy—it is rainy," as the case might be, but always said, " I shall be hot—I shall be cold—I shall be wet," in a manner entirely her own.

Monsieur Berthier preferred walking in the forest to coming in the carriage with us, and Monsieur Dessaix had music to write, and evidently thought that a day in the open air might be the death of him: so the driving party consisted solely of Madame Olympe and myself. At a little after eleven she came in, looking like a magnificent wall-flower, with a dark brown tweed dress shot with crimson, a deep orange-coloured silk handkerchief tied loosely round her throat, and a golden pheasant's wing in her hat. She had, as usual, her hands filled with flowers, but this time they were little nosegays of Parma violets, which she distributed to Ursula, Jeanne, Monsieur de Saldes, and Monsieur Charles, who were all going to ride, and who stuck them into the button-holes of their coats and habits. The

open carriage came to the door at half-past eleven.
Ursula, at the last moment, had some slight
dispute with Monsieur de Saldes, and in her
habit, just as she was, she jumped into the carriage
with Madame Olympe and myself.

It was a splendid autumn morning. The
earth sparkled in every direction like precious
stones, the dew lay like diamonds in the grass,
and the air was full of floating gossamers (the
Virgin's threads, as they are called in France), as
we bowled down the hill to the river. Over the
great bridge we went, and straight at once into the
forest. It is all divided into long alleys, which
lead into large green open places, or *carrefours*,
from which six or seven different roads diverge,
and in the centre of which there is an enormous
sign-post giving the direction of each. I should
have thought it impossible to find one's way without these, one path seemed so exactly to resemble
another; but Madame Olympe told me that the
gentlemen were often out after nightfall, and
managed to pilot themselves successfully even
when it was far too dark to read what was written
on the posts.

It was an enchanting drive to the place of

rendezvous. Generally the wood lay packed away on each side of the open roads. The trees were not large, as in our forests, but slender young slips, growing all close together, through which driving would have been impossible, and walking, for the most part difficult and unpleasurable; but one looked into depths of delicate leaves, until the whole atmosphere seemed to be a sort of pale transparent glowworm-green, as one rolled along with gentle motion and noiseless wheels over the yielding sand. Sometimes we drove for a long way under large trees through the very heart of the forest. In one place all the boles of the trees were covered with lichen; they looked like metal shafts of some strange gnome palace. Here we went along with a soft crushing sound over precious emerald mosses and the red gold of fallen beech-leaves; the whole air filled with delicious autumn savours, musky gusts of a wild woodland odour, and the bitter fragrance of bruised leaves. At last we got to the *carrefour*, or place of the rendezvous, and drew up before the door of a little country inn, where we saw the men and dogs who had been seeking out the track of the wild boar, and who had just arrived.

Two hours before daybreak these four men, with four dogs, go out with lanterns to seek the track; this is technically called the *aller au bois*. These hounds (*limiers*) are mute, and never follow the track of roebuck, rabbit, or hare. The forest is divided among them into four separate allotments, and each man with his dog explores the portion appointed for him, taking care never to interfere with the beat of the others. The next thing done is to *prendre les grands devants*. This consists in going round and round each division in ever-narrowing circles, until they come upon the track, or *brisée*, which takes its name from the custom of breaking a branch as soon as the trace is found—which branch they lay upon the ground with the point turned in the direction of the track. They then come back with their *limiers*, after a walk of about six hours, to the rendezvous (which generally takes place at twelve o'clock, or thereabouts), and dress themselves properly in the livery of the hunt.

By degrees, people on foot, and people on horseback, and people in open carriages began to assemble. The ladies, who all appeared to be more or less acquainted, got out of their various vehicles to speak to each other; and hairy men dismounted, or reined up, and bowed and talked to those ladies who remained in their carriages. There was one coachful of cousins from the village of Sept-Moulins, about four miles away from Marny; another with some smart ugly women, whom nobody knew, from the neighbouring town; one fat old lady was drawn by a couple of superb Percheron horses, small, robust, well-built animals of the old French post-horse breed, snow-white, with thick tails sweeping the ground, and powerful manes, that flew out to the wind like great sheets of silver in the sun: they were fiery, restive creatures, and looked splendid as they kept neighing and pawing the ground with impatience whenever they had to stand still for a single instant. Last of all arrived a sort of charming open *char-à-banc*, with pretty Madame Prévost, her kind-looking old husband, and a most absurd old friend, with a large red nose and a curly grey wig, who always lives with them, and whose name, I was told, was Hégésippe Gigonnet. Their carriage is a very popular one: it is laden with all sorts of good eatables, which are liberally distributed to the hungry,—and also with brandy, arnica, plaster, and other useful remedies, in case of any simple accident.

The ladies' dress was an extravagant imitation of the out-of-door costume of our own Englishwomen—the looped-up gown and coloured petticoat beneath; but in spite of every variety of rainbow tint which their gaudy skirts displayed, they presented a dowdy appearance, very different from the smart neat look which a well-appointed Englishwoman has when she is properly got up for walking. They wore ugly hats of fanciful shapes, but one felt at a glance that they were born to put nothing but Parisian bonnets of the latest fashion upon their heads, and to do no real out-of-door work. Presently Monsieur Charles, Monsieur de Saldes, and Jeanne came up, and then Monsieur Charles was informed of the different tracks that had been found by the *limiers*.

The servants of the hunt are called by picturesque names that all bear some reference to the sport. The huntsman or *piqueur* (pronounced *piqueux*) was called Latrace—his real name was Martin; there were five *valets-de-chien*, or whippers-in, on horseback, whose hunting names were La Rosée, La Feuille, Fanfare, La Brisée, La Broussaille; and there was one *valet-de-chien* on foot, who was called Tempête. La Broussaille and Tempête brought with them about sixty hounds to the meet: some of these dogs were French, but the greater proportion of them were fox-hounds got over from England. I jumped out of the carriage and went with Monsieur de Saldes to talk to them. They looked so natural and so sweet, with their heavy jaws and gentle eyes, waving their tails and making good-natured grumbling expostulations with fine bass voices.

Monsieur Charles having decided upon the track, about twenty out of the sixty were despatched in separate relays to different parts of the forest where the boar was supposed to be likely to pass. These hounds were older and rather slower than the others, and were called the old pack (*la vieille meute*). The forty remaining hounds were kept for following the track. Out of these, eight of the very best were selected to make the attack; the rest were divided into relays of about four couple, which were held in leashes by the *valets-de-chien*.

A Boar-hunt. 139

We now all got back into our carriages, and accompanied by a field of about fifty or sixty people began to move towards the spot where the beast was supposed to be. When we arrived there, the eight *chiens d'attaque* were put into the cover, followed by the huntsman on foot. We coasted along on the outside, guided by the rushing of the animals through the leaves, and the huntsman's cries of *Hou!—hou! Après! La voie!* (the right road). *Volcelet!* (here it is). Suddenly he caught sight of the boar and struck up the fanfare of the *sanglier* upon his horn, the dogs gave tongue, the gentlemen dashed off, blowing the *sanglier* with all their might, the *valets-de-chien* tore along, almost dragged off their horses by the pulling of the hounds in leash, and we set off at a hand-gallop followed by all the other carriages. It was a charming and a very varied spectacle. There was none of the uniformity of get-up that characterizes an English field: every one had turned out in different costume; most of the gentlemen of the neighbourhood, who were personal friends of Monsieur Charles, wore his white uniform with the maroon facings; then there were men in all sorts of cut-away and fly-away coats—some in elaborate suits of velveteen knickerbockers; a party of cuirassiers quartered in the neighbouring town appeared in regimentals, and bumped along after the boar in true *haute-école* style.

Suddenly, at the end of one of the long alleys, we saw the boar leap across the road. It was a *ragot* or middle-sized one, the most dangerous sort of all. Immediately all the horns struck up the fanfare of the *ragot*, the tearing, dragging hounds were loosed at last from the leashes, and away we all pelted in full chase, the horns blowing the *volcelet* and the *bien-aller* with might and main. It was not English sport. I do not know if it was good sport; of this I was no judge, but the excitement of that morning rush through the great glades of the sunlit forest, with the music and the animation of the whole scene, was a thing never to be forgotten. Ursula's eyes were staring wide open for the first time in her life, and Madame Olympe was screaming at the top of her voice. At last they got before us and out of sight, and we lost the track, and stopped for about a quarter of an hour, listening in vain for the fanfare to guide us. We then drove wildly about the forest in every direction, sometimes faintly catching, sometimes losing again the sound of the horns in the distance. Once the coachman called out, and we all stood up in the carriage as a company of stags, startled by the noise, bounded grandly one after another across the road, right in front of us. We were entirely thrown out, and at last came to a halt in one of the green places, not knowing in the least which path to take. We waited here for about half an hour in great despondency, afraid that our day's sport was over, when suddenly Monsieur Charles, followed by Jeanne, Monsieur de Saldes, and five or six gentlemen, came galloping by, blowing the *débuché* as hard as he could. "To the left! to the left!" he shouted, as he flew past, and we wheeled round, and to the left we galloped too. The *débuché* meant that the beast had taken to the open. We followed full tilt, got at last to the border of the plain, and saw the boar cross it with the whole field in hot pursuit, and then madly dashing into the river, swim across to a small island in the middle, where he presently landed with the hounds in full cry at his heels, and was lost in the thicket. The sun was going down in a sea of molten gold as the horns played first the *bat l'eau* (gone to the water), and then the first half of the *halali*. The river gave back the forms of the men and horses and trees upon the bank with such transparent clearness that they seemed literally living over again in the water. What a scene it was—all loveliness and peace! I cannot say how the spectacle of the solemn dying day at once turned the current of my feelings, or how discordant and savage the cries of all those men, hunting a wretched animal to the death in the quiet face of nature, suddenly became to me. After a few minutes the poor beast emerged at the other end of the island, and still followed by his yelling persecutors, in despair took to the water a second time. Shot after shot was fired at him in vain, as he swam vigorously for the mainland. At last Latrace jumped into the stream as he neared the shore, and stabbed him with his hunting-knife *au défaut de l'épaule*, in the one vulnerable place—the joint just behind the shoulder—while the horns struck up the last part of the *halali*, which is never played until the boar is killed.

And then we all turned homeward, and under

that gentle sky I felt conscience-stricken, and rather as if I had been assisting at a murder. It was dark and coldish by the time we got back to the house, and very cheering and pleasant was that large room, bright with candle and fire light, and not less so the cup of tea that dear Madame Olympe made for us. Presently Jeanne, Monsieur Charles, and Monsieur de Saldes came dropping in. Jeanne came up and kissed me very affectionately, as I lay on my big sofa resting and talking to Ursula.

"How sweet you smell, child," said I.

"It is my violets," she answered. "They are quite fresh still."

"Bless me!" cried Ursula, "what can have become of mine? I have lost them! I suppose they must have tumbled down as I was getting in or out of the carriage.

She then left her chair, and went away in a very marked manner as Monsieur de Saldes brought me my tea and sat down by me to talk over the impression that French hunting had made upon me. He very good-naturedly told me a great deal more about it. Boars of all ages are hunted. There are the *marcassins* or babies, the *bêtes de compagnie* and *bêtes rousses* from six to eighteen months old—the *ragotin*, which is about eighteen months old—the *ragot* of two years old —the boar in his third year—the boar in his fourth year. Then there is the huge *solitaire*, who lives alone, and for whom they play the *royale fanfare*, the *solitaire miré* (an old fellow with his tusks turned down, so that he cannot toss the dogs), and the *laie*, or female, for whom the fanfare of the *meunière* is played.

The first half of the *halali* is played when the boar is at bay; the second when he is killed, and he is never killed until he has been at bay. There is also the *halali tenante*—when the boar at bay tosses some of the hounds and then begins running again. If the animal is very fierce, in order to save the hounds the gentlemen will sometimes dismount and prick him with their hunting-knives to cause a diversion. The boar then leaves the dogs and rushes at the men, and there is a general *sauve qui peut*—up trees or anywhere. Sometimes the men as well as the dogs get wounded. Last season Latrace had his leg ripped up by the boar's tusks, and was badly hurt. The cries of *vocelet* or *volcelet*, and *vlaut—vlaut!*

which are continually heard during the hunt, are corruptions of *voilà ce l'est, le voilà là haut.* The morning after the hunt the missing hounds are tracked out, and found wounded or dead. The men take other dogs with them, whose ears they pull to make them cry, and so attract their wounded and lost companions. The *limiers*, who find the first trace of the boar, are put into a cart and driven home from the meet by Madame Moreau—an old woman about the château who does every sort of job—sometimes goes to fetch letters and sometimes goes to fetch bread. We met her in the forest going back to Marny, with four or five of the great circular loaves of common household bread which the servants eat, slung like so many necklaces round her mahogany-coloured old throat.

When Ursula and I went up to dress for dinner we took no light with us, as we had fire and candles in our own room. At the head of the stair was Monsieur Berthier's room, and just beyond it was a swing-door, which one had to pass in order to get to Monsieur Dessaix's room and ours. On opening this we nearly knocked down Monsieur Jacques, who was standing hidden behind it, and who had not heard us approach.

"Oh! Jacques, have I hurt you?" exclaimed Ursula with concern, for it was she who had pushed the door. "But what are you doing there in the dark just behind the door?"

"It is abominable," he said in a whisper. "They do not love me here. I have had a miserable day—I have passed it (all of it!) behind this door. Have you seen his room?" he continued, indicating Monsieur Berthier's. "Have you seen how large it is? twice as large as mine! After you were gone this morning, he and I came upstairs to write. After a little while I heard him go down, and I thought I would peep into his room. I had only time just to see how nice and big it was—for crac! he was up again in a minute. I suppose he had only gone to put his letter in the box. So I jumped back and hid behind the door, and watched till he went down again, and then I took another peep. It is much, much nicer than mine! I have watched him go down three times, and each time I have seen some fresh nice thing that he has."

"What dreadful nonsense, Jacques," said Ursula.

"He has two jugs—a large one and a little one. I have only one small one."

"For shame!" she said indignantly. "How could you go into another person's room in that way?"

"And a tea-service, and a gilt Cupid on the top of his looking-glass."

She took him by the shoulder, and putting him into his own room, shut the door angrily upon his complaints.

The evening was spent chiefly in making out the programme for the Sunday's music. Ursula found that she could stick an "*O Salutaris*" upon the beginning of Stradella's song, which carried her through the first eight bars, after which she boldly merged into "ovunque il guardo io giro, cerco te, guardo te, sospiro," &c. I was sorry that she had determined to do it, but she seemed to look at the matter altogether from an artistic point of view, and as it was a Roman Catholic church, not to see any reason against it. And Madame Olympe's mind was entirely divided between her ecstacy at the notion of hearing Ursula's great voice and grand style in the ample space of a church—where they would have room to spread themselves—and her pleasure in the gratification which she knew it would give to the poor Curé to have such fine music for the occasion of his confirmation. Monsieur Jacques had been pacified by my representation that his coming had been altogether unexpected, and that Monsieur Berthier and Monsieur Kiowski were both in possession before his arrival ; and he entered with zeal into the details of the programme, and was of the greatest service in selecting and arranging the progression of the pieces. Monsieur Berthier, Monsieur de Saldes and I sat and talked together, and I made the former especially happy by translating for his benefit Ford's speech in the *Merry Wives of Windsor*—" Then she plots, then she ruminates, then she devises : and what they think in their hearts they may effect, they will break their hearts but they will effect." He was enchanted with this. "What a genius ! " he cried. " How he knows the heart of woman ! How he must have known the English woman ! " And nothing would serve but he must learn the sentiment by rote in the original tongue : after which he passed the whole evening saying at intervals, "Zen zey ruminaate, Zen zey *devaise*," and smiling contentedly to himself. The next day he left us for Paris, to the regret of every one, for he was so gentle and amiable that it was quite impossible not to like him. "And such a true gentleman," said Madame Olympe; "so unlike Lady Blankeney, with her eternal 'Countess' and 'Marquis.' She thinks it quite *Faubourg St. Germain* (to use her own favourite expression), whereas it is precisely Faubourg St. Germain that never does it. Prince or Princesse are the only titles ever given in addressing people—everything under that rank is simply spoken to as Monsieur or Madame de So-and-So."

"But," said I, "does not Jeanne always call Monsieur Charles Marquis?"

"Yes," she replied, "but that is her sauciness—a sort of little nickname, as boys in England call their father 'governor,'—nothing more."

In the afternoon Madame Olympe took me over in her pony-chair to Sept-Moulins. Said she: "We have had a specimen of an English institution in Maria Blankeney—I will now show you one of a French institution."

After a very pretty drive of about three-quarters of an hour, we arrived at the château. It was a picturesque old place, in the middle of a very good imitation of an English park, and surrounded by a broad moat, filled with water. Luckily they were all at home, and we were let in. The first person I was presented to was Monsieur Henri de Caradec, the master of the house—an amiable, courteous old man in his hundredth year, in the possession of all his faculties, and having preserved to that venerable age that rarest of all faculties—the power of loving and of being loved. He lives here with his sweet old wife, who, being only eighty-four, is looked upon by him almost as a child. Nothing ever was more charming than the tender attachment of these dear old people: everything said by the one has reference to the other; and they cannot be happy for five minutes out of each other's sight. Living under the same roof with them are Monsieur Octave de Caradec, their eldest son, and his wife, Madame de Lanneray (Monsieur Octave's eldest daughter), with her handsome young husband and their little Thérèse of four years old, and Mademoiselle Marie de

Caradec, her unmarried sister, a young woman of about twenty, with a delightful countenance. Madame de Beaumont, Monsieur Henri's only daughter, a widow, with a grown-up son, also inhabits the château.

When we came away I asked Madame Olympe if it was the general custom in France for families to live in this patriarchal manner, and if it worked successfully? She said that the custom was almost universal, and that as to its working, no doubt there were occasional disputes and differences, since where humanity is offence must needs come; but that on the whole the families so united generally lived happily together, and were strongly attached to each other. Certainly I had hardly ever seen anything so charming as that old man playing with his little great-grandchild, and I must confess that it seems to me both pious and natural to crown old age with fresh garlands of spring, rather than as we do in England, when the blossoms and leaves have all dropped off, to leave it naked and alone to die.

As we drove home Madame Olympe talked a great deal about Monsieur de Saldes, much of his gifts and accomplishments, and more still of the wretched manner in which he had thrown them all away. " With his talents," she said, " he might have distinguished himself in a thousand ways; he has had opportunity after opportunity offered him of doing something with his life, but he is utterly devoid of ambition, and his supreme indolence and consistent system of self-indulgence have induced him steadily to reject them all. It has ended with isolating him a good deal, for while his real taste for art and science renders the usual run of men in his own position of life wearisome and distasteful to him, his want of application and concentration, and a certain inconvenient fastidiousness and capriciousness of temperament, prevent him from associating with people of another class who would interest him. He is a pedant among fashionable men, and a man of fashion among the learned, and so he remains like the Halb-Hexe in *Faust*, suspended between earth and heaven and fit for neither—helpless, hurtful, and charming!"

I told her of Monsieur Jacques' terror about Ursula and Monsieur René. She laughed and remarked that she did not think that he need be under any sort of apprehension on that score, for that Ursula's manner to Monsieur de Saldes always indicated the most perfect indifference, while his to her seemed almost to express antipathy.

"You are the person who appears to have captivated him, my dear Bessy," she said, and added, "If your mother had not told me of your engagement, my dear child, I should have felt a little anxious and nervous about it; conquests over René are worse than defeats. Ah! isn't it sad to think that with all his power and all his charm, his progress through life will have been marked by nothing but the tears of a few women who have loved him?"

"Dear Madame Olympe," I answered, "I, as you know, bear a charmed life; but are you never afraid for Jeanne? she is very fond of him, and he is so attractive, and so often here!"

"Yes," answered Madame Olympe; "but Jeanne is a wonderful child: her acute observation and the justness of her mind are quite remarkable. Thank God, she has little imagination, and abundant common sense and principle, and when she does love, it will be a good man. Fancy her coming to me the other day and saying with the utmost gravity, 'Send for the doctor, maman—René is ill. Baptiste was despatched early this morning for the curé, and he has been closeted with him for the last half hour. René has no doubt had his *crampes* badly in the night."

"Monsieur René is not much given to religious observance, I imagine?" said I.

"Only, as Jeanne says, when he has his *crampes*. He is never religious but when he has an indigestion, and then he becomes superstitious."

In the evening Madame Martin (Latrace's little wife of seventeen) came up with two or three young girls from the village to try her duet with Jeanne, and some of the choruses which were to be performed on Sunday. Madame Olympe accompanied, and Monsieur Jacques was indefatigable in helping to teach them all their parts. I, as usual, lay on my sofa talking to Ursula on one side and to Monsieur de Saldes on the other.

"To-morrow is the meet of the staghounds," said he. "Shall you go to it, Miss Hope?"

"No," said I, laughing, "I think not. I have not quite got over the emotion of yesterday's sport yet."

"Good heavens!" cried Ursula, "how I wish I could go. But there will be nothing all day but rehearsing, I suppose, and it will be out of the question."

"I like you for not liking it," continued Monsieur René, smiling charmingly at me, and taking no notice whatever of Ursula's speech. "It would not be womanly—it would not be *you* to take pleasure in putting anything to death."

"Are you fond of no sort of sport, Bessy?" said Ursula. "Do you never fish?"

"No," I said. "I tried once, but I was such a dreadful fool that I could neither put the worms on nor take the fish off the hook, and so I thought I had better not try again."

"I love it!" she said. "I am sure one is born a sportsman just as one is born a poet or a painter, or anything else. I could fish from morning to night, and shooting is more exciting still."

"Shooting!" said I. "Can you shoot, Ursula? Do you mean to say that you know how to shoot?"

"Yes," she answered, "and I delight in it. I shot at the country place of some friends of mine in Italy, and was quite clever at bringing down my hares and rabbits—running, I beg to state, not sitting. It's the best fun in the world!"

"Do you also consider it good fun, Miss Hamilton, when you manage to wound your game without killing it!" asked Monsieur de Saldes in his gentle voice.

"Well," answered she, coolly, "perhaps that is not quite so pleasant, but one gives them a little tap on the head with the wrong end of the gun, you know" (and she clacked her tongue against her palate), "and that soon puts them out of their pain." I saw that she had felt the inimical tone of his remark, and that her spirit was up.

"Luckily for me," said Monsieur de Saldes, "I am generally a dead shot. My nerve is inferior to yours, Miss Hamilton" (and he bowed). "Although I am a man, I have never yet been able to give a wounded creature that little tap you speak of."

"You prefer pampering your own squeamishness?" inquired she, innocently.

I, who had seen her quite unable to kill a wasp in our bed-room only the night before, knew she did not mean a word of what she was saying, but that she was stung by his contemptuous manner, and getting into one of her defiant moods.

So I endeavoured to start another subject, and asked her if she did not intend to try her voice in the church before singing there on Sunday.

"O dear, yes!" she said. "We are to have a grand rehearsal there to-morrow. How I do wish it was a theatre instead of a church, and that I was going to sing to a dear good honest paying public that could hiss me if it chose!"

Monsieur de Saldes' face expressed unmitigated disgust. "You once seriously entertained some thought of going on the stage, did you not?" said he. "I am afraid it has cost you a great deal to give it up?"

"More than you can conceive," she replied, complacently looking up at him from under her half-shut eyelids. "I cannot imagine anything more honourable than to work for one's bread, or anything more delightful than to earn it by civilizing and refining a sympathizing multitude."

"It must be gratifying, indeed," said he, "to pass one's evenings exposed to the gaze of every idiot who chooses to pay his half-crown for his stare, and equally delightful to spend one's days in the society of profligate and uneducated vagabonds."

"Ah, yes—I haven't tried profligacy yet," said Ursula, getting beyond all bounds in her desire to anger him. "But I must own that I find virtue uncommonly difficult, and upon the whole rather tiresome. With regard to vagabonds, I think when you made your last civil observation, it must have escaped your memory that my mother was one of the vagabonds in question, and that in preferring the company of people of genius to the exhausted atmosphere which appears to suit your complaint, I only chasse de race."

"Do you know this?" he said, with a most audacious smile, taking up a *Don Juan* that was lying on the table, and turning the title on the back carelessly towards her.

"You forget yourself—how dare you!" said Ursula, and she rose up opposite to him in a frenzy of indignation.

"When a woman does not respect herself, Miss Hamilton," he quietly replied, "she can hardly expect that other people will respect her."

She looked steadily at him for a few seconds while she struggled to say something; but no sound would come, and her lips quivered, and her eyes closed: she then grew deadly white and left the room. "Oh, you hit too hard!" I exclaimed in despair. "You have hurt her!"

"Hurt her!" he echoed. "I think she must be gone mad! Hurt her? I hope I have—it is quite the kindest thing left for one to do by her."

I gathered up my work hastily and was going to follow her, when Monsieur de Saldes continued: "You are so young, so pure, so good, you do not know the face of evil, as a poor battered wretch like myself does. I implore you break off your intimacy with Ursula; she is no fit companion for you—indeed she is not. Depend upon it, that when a woman of her years already finds virtue wearisome, the chances are that before long she will find it impossible!"

"Monsieur René," said I, "for shame! Your dislike is making you do her far less than justice"—and I got up from the sofa. "I, who have known her less long, know her better than you do!"

"Don't go—don't go, I beseech you," he said,

"or I shall never forgive myself. I believe the truth is that I absolutely loathe that woman!" and he ground his teeth.

I made no answer and was passing on, meaning to leave the room quietly, when Madame Olympe —who was standing up behind Monsieur Jacques' chair and beating time while he accompanied Jeanne's duet—suddenly caught me round the waist and held me fast, while she went on counting her "Un, deux, trois;" and so I stayed and grew calm as I listened. "Ave sanctissima, mater amabilis, ora, ora pro nobis!" sang the two thin childish voices. It was wonderfully pure and passionless, and I wished my poor Ursula could have heard it.

When I went upstairs she was in bed. I went close up, but she did not stir. Her thick fringes of eyelashes were all matted together in little wet points, and the marks of tears still lay in wet lines all down her face. She had gone to sleep crying, with a small iron cross which had belonged to her mother—and which she always wore next her skin—grasped tightly in one of her hands.

When I came down on Saturday morning,

I found Madame Olympe busily reading a despatch which had just arrived from the Sœur Marie.

"Just look at it," she said, putting it into my hands. "And tell me if you ever read anything more grotesque and grim than this cake-and-death joke?" The letter was as follows:—

"Madame la Comtesse will be glad, no doubt, to learn that Madame Simon is still in the same state. The difficulty of swallowing remains very great. She only took one small teacupful of broth, by spoonfuls, at intervals all through the whole of yesterday; still there is no change for the worse. Yesterday, after we had made her comfortable for the night, Madame Chevet, the nurse, said to me, 'She will be in the other world before to-morrow.' But I was certain that her hour was not yet come, and so I laid a wager with her about it. The stake was a *galette*, and I have won it, since here is to-morrow and Madame Simon is still alive. We did it, Madame la Comtesse, to amuse ourselves a little while we were watching. Madame la Comtesse need send no money at present. I looked into Madame

Simon's purse while she was asleep, and saw in it two bank-notes,—one for two hundred francs and another for one hundred.—Madame la Comtesse's devoted and obedient servant,

"Sœur Marie."

"Would one not believe from this," said Madame Olympe, when I gave her back her letter, "that the poor old sister was a regular Mrs. Gamp? Yet no one ever was tenderer or more devoted than she is to all those who suffer. It is a strange childish element that I have observed in many of the sisters of charity and in many of the country priests too."

"Has Monsieur Kiowski arrived?" asked Monsieur Charles, as we sat down to breakfast.

"Not yet. But he will be here directly," answered Madame Olympe.

"If he comes at all," said Monsieur de Saldes.

"Do you think he will not come?" asked Monsieur Charles. "Well, I am a little of your opinion. To come all the way across the sea (and there was such a high wind in the night too!) to sing a trio, seems a strong measure."

"He will come," said Jeanne.

"He will come," said Madame Olympe.

"He will come," said Ursula.

"What faith!" said Monsieur de Saldes. "Happy man to be so believed in! But you have said nothing." And he turned to me. "What is your opinion? Do you believe that he will come?"

Just then there was a great bustle outside, and we heard a high voice asking breathlessly if we were all well and if we were in the breakfast-room. The door was thrown open, and Monsieur Kiowski appeared. He looked pale and tired. He had been travelling all night and had had a rough passage; but he had sold his friend's *Egeria*, and, true to his word, there he was to sing the *Tantum ergo*. He was received with acclamations.

Our whole day was passed in rehearsing. We went to the church after breakfast, and returned there again in the afternoon. The piano, which was sent down from the château, was too large to go up the small staircase of the tribune opposite the high altar, where the singing was to take place, and the noise and bustle of the workmen who hauled it up by ropes from the body of the church rather jarred upon my nerves. So I stayed below as far from it all as I could, and amused myself with reading a catechism which had been left upon one of the chairs.

Monsieur de Saldes declined going into the tribune, where Madame Olympe had called him, and came and sat near the high altar with me. This I was convinced he did to avoid Ursula. He and she had kept carefully apart from each other all day; to me she never once mentioned him, nor made the slightest allusion to his behaviour of the night before. Her manner was grave, quiet, and unexceptionable; but her whole aspect was one of concentrated pride, and I saw that she had been deeply offended.

The singers kept themselves warm with singing I suppose, but I was frozen when the afternoon rehearsal was over and we all came out; and having got my clogs on, I made up my mind to walk across the fields home. Monsieur René, who was cold too, offered to escort me.

He seemed very sad, and I was obliged to recollect his really prosperous circumstances not to feel myself full of sympathy for unexisting misfortune. He spoke of a life hopeless and aimless, a failure from beginning to end, and was so gentle, so depressed, and so loveable, that I felt myself overflowing with pity for him, until I remembered what Madame Olympe had told me of his determined rejection of all employment and of every sort of career. I was glad when we got home, for he was altogether so touching about himself that, in a few minutes more, I am sure he would have made me cry—although I knew perfectly well that it was all humbug.

Monsieur Jacques came into the hall and began speaking to me, as I was trying to undo one of my clogs. I could not unclasp it, and Monsieur de Saldes knelt down to help me. As he stooped, a bunch of dead violets fell out of his breast. He hastily picked them up and thrust them back again, and I believe thought that Monsieur Jacques and I—who were talking together—had not perceived them; but we both had certainly the same idea, for as soon as he had left us Monsieur Jacques called to me as I was going upstairs, and said again, in an agonized whisper, "Do not let Ursula marry him!"

"Why don't you marry her yourself?" said I, laughing. "That would settle it all comfortably."

He looked up at me with a sharp gaze of far-seeing misery.

"She would wash me—and I should die!" he said.

In the evening the village-girls came up again to the house, and the music was worked at indefatigably. When we went to bed, I sat down in an arm-chair by the fire, and began building up the bits of wood and making a blaze. Ursula presently came and knelt down by me, and after a few minutes' silence said to me, "Bessie, though I have not known you long, I love you so much that I want to take an immense liberty with you."

"Take it, my dear," I answered, kissing her upturned forehead. "I hardly know what you can have to say to me that demands so solemn a preface."

She coloured slightly, and after a minute's hesitation said, quickly and nervously, "Don't let René de Saldes persuade you that he is fond of you."

"My dear child!" I exclaimed, much surprised.

"It is his way," she continued, "and he is not trustworthy. Don't let him do it!"

"Do you mean," said I, "that it is his way to persuade people that he is fond of them, when he really does not care at all about them?"

"I don't know that," she answered. "I have seen him very successfully make people think so about whom he did not care at all; and I have seen him like people too, as he does you; but, on the whole, those he liked, I think, came even worse off than those he didn't. You see he can only love just a very little himself; and he is always loved a great deal, and you mustn't love him, dear Bessie—indeed you mustn't. You cannot think how the notion of your being made unhappy by him has afflicted and tormented me."

"Don't be anxious about it any more, dear," said I. "Why, at all events, you know I am going away on Monday."

"Yes," she replied; "but to whom? to what? to a narrow circle of exhausting and ungrateful duties, and perhaps with a heart made heavy by the remembrance of what you have left behind. Ah! I cannot bear to think of it!" and she flung her arms round me.

She was so full of affectionate solicitude, that

I determined to put her mind altogether at ease about me.

"Dear Ursula," I said, "I am going home to some one who is not like Monsieur de Saldes; some one who is able, thank heaven, to love a great deal, and who loves me as much as he is able." I then told her of my engagement to Mr. L'Estrange.

"No, really, dear Bessie!" she exclaimed. "Are you really engaged? How very, very glad I am that it is all right! and is he very charming, dear? and should I like him? and would he like me? and do you love him very, very much, dear?"

"He is very learned and very clever, and quite the most charming person I ever met," I answered. "And he is so strong and gentle and good, that it is impossible not to love him."

"And how long have you been engaged to him, dear Bessie?" she asked, eagerly.

I could not help feeling rather sad as I told her that we had been engaged ever since I was seventeen.

"Good gracious, what a long time!" she exclaimed. "Why, how long is it? how old are you?"

"I am twenty-eight, my dear," I answered with a little sigh.

"Twenty-eight! impossible!" she cried. "Why, I always fancied you were younger than I am."

I laughed and said that little whitey-brown women with unsalient features always looked younger than they really were.

"Then you have been engaged eleven whole years? Good gracious, how very awful!" she exclaimed. "Why didn't you marry?"

"Because William is only a poor curate, dear, and could not afford to keep a wife," I answered.

"But when are you going to marry? directly, now? as soon as ever you get back?"

I told her that there was no possibility of our marrying until he got some preferment: that at present he had only a hundred and fifty pounds a year, and that of course he could not support a wife upon that income.

"Good gracious!" she began again. "Then after losing the eleven best years of your life, you are actually going to wait for perhaps another eleven? Good gracious, what a dismal state of things!" and she sat down on the ground, with her hands clasped round her knees, looking into the red embers.

"My dear," said I, "I have not lost these eleven years, since I have passed them in loving the best and noblest human creature that I ever knew." Nevertheless, Ursula's discouraging view of the case affected me more than I was willing to own. It did seem rather hopeless—and she rang the changes on it in a way that was painful to me in spite of all her real kindness and my affection for her.

"Good gracious!" she ejaculated, thoughtfully to herself, still looking into the fire. "And isn't he likely to get some preferment soon?"

"Indeed I cannot tell," said I. "They know how distinguished and how hard-working he is,—perhaps something may turn up before very long."

"But eleven whole years! Good gracious, my dear, I don't see my way at all! What will you do if he doesn't get any preferment?" she continued after a pause.

"Wait on, I suppose," I said, rather drearily, and I began not to see my way either—so I got into bed as quickly as I could, and pretended to be asleep, that she might leave off saying " Good gracious!" at my unprosperous little love-affair any more.

Our Sunday function went off very brilliantly, and was eminently successful. The church was crammed from one end to the other with the relations and friends of the young people who were the principal objects of interest in the ceremony. I found that it was not a confirmation service, but the taking of their first communion by the young village children who had just been confirmed. And what with the part they took and the part that we took in the performance, I must say that I think it was altogether as unedifying a spectacle as I ever assisted at. Our programme was singular but effective.

First came the glorious *Tantum ergo*, for which Monsieur Kiowski had sacrificed himself with such a good grace, and which went beautifully—Monsieur Jacques, with a roll of music for a bâton, directing for all the world as though we had been in a theatre. Then Ursula sang her Marcello psalm, and the grave tones went surging over the church in great waves of sound and sending shivers down one's spine. Then followed a trio—also by Marcello—sung by Ursula, Monsieur Kiowski, and Monsieur Charles: this too was beautiful and perfectly devout. After it came Jeanne's and Madame Martin's sweet hymn to the Virgin; then a cantique by the village-girls, as trivial and profane as the romances one hears upon the street organs, and very like them; then Ursula got up again and sang her Stradella love-song, transmogrified for the first three or four bars into an *O Salutaris*, and then suddenly flaming out into very earthly ecstasies in right good Italian. Fortunately it was a song with a Da capo to it, so that she was able to relapse into devotion and Latin again at the conclusion. It was a splendid piece of audacity, and a splendid piece of art; but although I could not help being transported with it, my conscience kept putting up a regretful protest all the time, and I could not bear her doing it. However, she had never been taught anything but singing, and religion has to be learnt as well as everything else. The performance wound up with a quartet (the most serious they could find,) out of Rossini's *Tancredi*, sung, without any attempt at disguise, in its native Italian. Mixed up with all this came bits of the regular mass music, executed in our tribune (but not by us) upon a little braying, fiendish old organ with about as much regard to time and tune as distinguishes the infant German band in London streets. Alternating with it came doleful gusts of nasal chaunting from the officiating priests below. No one appeared to have the slightest idea what was the right moment for anything to take place, and we made three or four false starts, cropping out into *O Salutarises* and *Amabilises* upon improper occasions, and being rebuked for it and speedily reduced to silence by Monsieur le Curé, who kept up a series of mysterious telegraphic communications with us, by means of his arms, from the other end of the church, where he was (I suppose) praying at the high altar. Sometimes he graciously waved and beckoned; at other times he protested, and, as it were, thrust us back again into our seats; and once or twice he did something that looked uncommonly like shaking his fist at us, when we persisted in opening our mouths in the wrong place. His energetic and expressive movements were all we had to guide us, and I think it was wonderful that the music did not go worse astray.

Then there were long orations made by two poor little girls in their white communion-frocks, who took it by turns to stand up in the crowded church, accusing themselves of the most frightful iniquities, and addressing long pompous harangues to the priest, to their parents, to the assistant spectators, to their companions, to the Virgin, to God; which were declaimed with the most laboured gestures—evidently perfectly unspontaneous, and bearing no reference whatever to the words they were uttering.

"Vous me voyez prosternée," was asserted by one child, standing bolt upright, who, poor little soul, proceeded to inform us, "qu'elle avait perdu la robe de son innocence," and invited us with continual placid wavings of her arms, a shrill voice and cheerful countenance, to "écouter ses sanglots" and "contempler ses larmes." These recitations were relieved by a most remarkable set of evolutions—a sort of military entertainment without fire-arms—precipitately performed at intervals by all the little boys to the sound of a wooden clapper played by the priest; but the drilling had been incomplete, and the execution was rather agitated and leaving something to be desired. It was inexpressibly comical—but, at the same time and on that very account, extremely painful and disagreeable. It went to my heart to see children, in themselves sacred, and doing so sacred a thing, going through a series of antics which made them look like so many absurd little parrots and apes. Ursula received many compliments as she went out, and people told her how much impressed they had been with the devotional feeling of what she had sung : her part of the business seemed the most solemn after all.

"Come, get in, get in!" cried Madame Olympe, who had gone on before us, and who was already seated in the carriage. "We must make haste if we mean to go on the river before it gets dark."

"I jumped in, Ursula jumped in, Monsieur Charles climbed up to the box ; Jeanne, Monsieur Dessaix and Monsieur Kiowski had already started walking—taking the short cut across the fields.

"Is there room for me?" asked Monsieur de Saldes. He had before said that he meant to walk, which was what I saw had determined Ursula upon driving.

"Yes, yes, there is plenty of room ; get in!"

said Madame Olympe. He got in, and as he did so on one side, Ursula got out on the other. " But what are you doing ? " asked Madame Olympe, rather impatiently.

" Only going to run after Jeanne and Jacques," said Ursula, setting off. " My feet got quite frozen in that cold tribune, and I want to warm them."

" There's room inside," shouted Madame Olympe, through the front window, to Monsieur Charles; he had no great-coat, and she thought he would be cold. " Get into the carriage and let the servant go upon the box."

" But, Olympe, I am quite comfortable up here," he answered.

" Get into the carriage."

" I have got a shawl over my knees," said he, appealingly.

" Get into the carriage."

" I was just going to smoke a little cigarette," he observed, mildly.

" But when I tell you to get into the carriage ! " she answered, her voice working up ominously towards the treble key.

He did as he was bid, and we started. After we had gone steadily along for about ten minutes, one of the horses shied at a piece of paper that was lying in the road. Madame Olympe gave a scream : " It's the white horse !" cried she.

" It's the bay one," said Monsieur René, looking out.

The coachman whipped and whipped in vain; the animal jumped and fidgeted, but would not go by the place.

Madame Olympe was beginning to be a good deal frightened. " It's the white horse!" she exclaimed again.

Monsieur Charles now looked out in his turn. " No, Olympe," said he, " it is the bay horse."

" It's the white horse!" she vociferated, eyeing him despotically, between two screams. The beast now began to kick and plunge, and Madame Olympe got into a state of the most imperious terror.

" There is no white horse at all in the carriage," said Monsieur Charles.

" But when I tell you that I choose that it should be a white horse!" cried she in her highest key, and with her eyebrows running straight up her forehead into her hair. It was too funny, and we all went into fits of laughter, in which she could not help joining very heartily herself, in spite of her alarm. The gentlemen then got down, the restive creature was led past the obstacle, and presently we arrived safely at the water's edge, where we found the others waiting for us.

We jumped into the boat, and pushed off from shore : Monsieur de Saldes and Jeanne rowed We were all very quiet; some of us were a little exhausted by the exertions of the morning, and all were depressed by the feeling that it was the last of our many happy excursions. What an evening it was! One whole side of the heavens was of a deep solemn rose-colour, with a wondrous diaper of red brown leaves embroidered upon it by the branches of a screen of trees which stood out in strong relief against it : the other side was a blaze of golden fire. This effect lasted the longest : it only seemed to grow into an ever-deepening amber, haunting that half of heaven like some brooding passionate regret, while the rose hue passed first into violet, then into dark purple, and then faded away into still silver grey. Soft opal tints came down from the skies and lay upon the face of the waters, as we rowed away from all the glory into a world of delicate twilight

DRIFTING.

shadow. Suddenly, from the grey bank, burned out a single orange-coloured leaf. Oh! who shall explain the strange mystery by which one feels stabbed to the heart with a sharp pang of delight at some unexpected apparition of this kind? We all called aloud in one unanimous voice of salutation, as we floated past the little lonely flame. Presently the surface of the river became black as liquid ebony, the moon got up, and a pleasant rhythm of plashing oars, always accompanied by a bright flash of light, was all that marked our gentle progress through the water.

"Ah! Will no one sing and make this quite, quite perfect?" said Madame Olympe.

Monsieur Kiowski began the well-known air of the Sorrento boatmen, the *Fata d'Amalfi*, and Ursula joined in a second. While they sang, Jeanne and René pulled in their oars, and we went drifting—drifting—drifting along in soft darkness, listening to the passionate southern sounds. I could not help thinking that, perhaps when I am dying, that solitary leaf will burn into my heart once more, as I drift silently with closed eyes into the waters of the other life.

Every one felt grieved when Madame Olympe

unwillingly gave the signal for pulling to shore. The place where we landed was very shallow, and one had to step over large stepping-stones in the water in order to reach the bank. There was neither difficulty nor danger, and we accomplished it with perfect ease. Suddenly a plaintive voice was heard calling upon us all to stop. It was Monsieur Jacques, who had remained behind unperceived, and who now announced that it was simply impossible for him to get out of the boat or over the stones. It was quite in vain that we reasoned with him, and assured him that nothing could be easier: he stood there wailing and imploring without making the least attempt to move, until Madame Olympe, touched with compassion, strode down the bank again, recrossed the stones, and whipping him up round the knees like a baby, brought him in her arms triumphantly through the water back to us.

Monsieur Kiowski left us almost as soon as we returned to the house, very amiably sorry that he could not wait to escort me on my journey, but promising to come very soon and be presented to mother in town. The dinner was dreary—the cloud of last moments was upon us: Madame

Olympe hardly spoke; there seemed to be a sort of impassable wall built up between Ursula and Monsieur de Saldes; and Jeanne was miserable at losing us all. Monsieur Dessaix had a swelled face and went to bed before dinner. When we had gone back into the drawing-room, Madame Olympe began turning over our photograph-books. In looking through Ursula's she came upon a photograph of Colonel Hamilton, and looked at it with great interest for some time. She had not seen him for many years before his death. She then asked Ursula if she had no likeness of her mother; she said she had a miniature of her, and went to fetch it. When she showed it to us, I was struck with the unlikeness of the expression to her own. The colouring was the same, and so were the drooping lids; but the mouth looked all tremulous with tenderness, and I was at a loss to account for the sarcastic turn of Ursula's lips, until she showed us a small head of an Italian uncle of hers, a brother of her mother's, and I saw at once where it came from. We had nothing whatever of an evening. At about half-past ten, Madame Olympe said she had a headache, and folding me in her arms with a most maternal embrace, bade me farewell. I had to be off at four in the morning in order to catch the tidal train, and so we separated early, and indeed, with our opposed elements and dispositions of mind, it was quite the best thing to be done.

After Ursula and I had been some time in our room, it suddenly occurred to me that Madame Olympe had never given me a small parcel which she wished me to take over to England for her: so slipping on my dressing-gown I ran down by a back staircase which communicated directly with her apartment, to see about it. I cannot say how glad I am that it had so happened, for I had a last five minutes with her, so affectionate and tender that I would not have lost them for all the world. Just as I had bid her good-night for the second time, I recollected having left my photograph-book in the drawing-room, and as Madame Olympe assured me that no one was there, I ran through a little passage which led straight from her room into the drawing-room, to look for it, or rather to feel for it. I had no candle, but I knew perfectly well where I had left it,—on the top of the music-stand behind the curtain in the bay window—and I had just laid my hand upon it and felt its clasps, when I saw a sudden light through the chink of the curtain, and Ursula and Monsieur de Saldes came in together.

"You have come down for your mother's miniature?" said he.

"Yes, I left it on the chimney-piece," she answered calmly, going towards the fireplace.

"It is there no longer," he said. "I have got it." I took it because I knew you would come down for it, and because I wanted to speak to you. All day I have endeavoured to get near you, but your systematic avoidance of me rendered it impossible; now you must hear me. For the last two days, for what reason God alone knows, you have appeared to take a strange delight in presenting yourself under the most repulsive and unfavourable aspect. You have expressed feelings in every way discreditable to you, and in words that, if you remember them, might make you blush. I now come to tell you that all this I am willing to overlook, to believe that it was temper—caprice—excitability—whatever name you choose to give it, and I ask you to become my wife."

I never was more stupefied in my life than

when I found myself the involuntary recipient of this extraordinary confidence. However, I thought it so essential that these two should understand each other, that I quietly sat down in my corner, determined not for the world to move or interrupt them. Anything like the insolence of his tone and manner it was impossible to conceive. I was at a loss to imagine how she would answer him.

"Your wife?" said Ursula. The words dropped with awful calmness into the silence of the night.

"Yes," he continued, in the same tone of aggressive arrogance. "I am well aware how terribly against you your birth and education have been, but I make the just allowance for it, and remember that partly to these disadvantages and peculiar circumstances you also owe your strong individuality—which, while it is your snare, is also one of your most powerful attractions."

"Then," she said, with the most perfect composure, "I am to understand that you overlook my unfortunate antecedents and are willing to marry me on account of my originality? This is no doubt very kind, and highly flattering to me; but I think perhaps it might prove a dangerous experiment to both of us. Why, how little you know yourself, Monsieur de Saldes! Having married me for my unlikeness to other women, your first endeavour would be carefully to stamp out all the sharp corners of that individuality which has at present the good fortune to please you, and to blur me down into the dead level of everybody else. Failing to do this, as you would —for I am not made of very malleable stuff—you would soon get to hate me for the very thing that made you like me; after which I should probably have the gratification of seeing you devoted to some other woman immeasurably my inferior—a *Sophie de Malan!*" (this she said with unutterable contempt), "whose principal attraction would probably consist in her utter unlikeness to myself. No: I am sensible of the honour you do me, but I think the hazard too great and must decline it; and since a vagabond I am, a vagabond I will remain."

"It is you that do yourself injustice, not I," he replied with warmth. "It is you that say these hard things of yourself, not I. Should I ask you to be my wife if I did not know your real worth? It is this that drives me distracted to see you (*you!*) living with the sort of people you do, exposed to the odious familiarities of a Dessaix——"

"I do not know what reason you may have for speaking of Monsieur Dessaix with such sovereign contempt," she said. "I have myself the greatest admiration for him, not only on account of his remarkable genius, but for the sake of his disinterested nature and the generous self-denial of his whole life. When at his father's death his two young sisters were thrown entirely upon his hands, he was engaged to a woman to whom he was passionately attached. He broke off his engagement and gave up all thoughts of marriage, in order to educate and provide for his sisters. After years of self-abnegation and hard labour he has had the gratification of seeing them both honourably married, but his own existence has been entirely sacrificed. Who are you, Monsieur de Saldes, that you despise this man? Whom have you lived to benefit? whom have you worked to serve?"

"I beg your pardon," he answered, "if I have spoken of your friend in a way that has hurt your feelings. I have not the slightest doubt that he is a most estimable person; but *you* are altogether of another order——"

"I have no desire whatever to repudiate my class,—the class to which my mother belonged," she said very quietly. "And that being the case, you must perceive how totally unfit I am for the honour you propose to me."

"But don't you see," he rejoined eagerly, "that your marriage with me at once places you in an entirely different sphere—the one for which nature intended you? All these miserable antecedents and odious surroundings, which make me so utterly wretched, would by the force of circumstances die a natural death. Your marriage with me would at once remove you from them."

"I see," said Ursula, slowly. "And I should give up my dear old Giambattista, who, when my father was dead and I was left alone in our wretched lodging, came and fetched me away and brought me home to his old wife, and housed, and fed, and clothed me, as if I had been his own child. And I should also, no doubt, give up Jacques, who nursed me through that terrible small-pox, when even my own father was afraid to come near me, and I, neglected and forlorn, was left to toss with fever and worry through as I might;—Jacques, who sat up night after night with me, fanning me, and putting little bits of ice into my dry mouth, as my mother might have done. The first day that I felt better I insisted on his bringing me a looking-glass. Shall I ever forget it? I burst into tears of despair; and Jacques, while the tears ran down his own cheeks, took my hands and said, 'Do not weep. Thy soul is not changed. Thou wilt be always lovely to thy friends!' You, I remember, brought me a veil, and begged me to wear it when you called; the alteration in my complexion affected your finer sensibility so painfully. No, Monsieur de Saldes, I am properly alive to the compliment that you have paid me; but I am afraid I might find the conditions hard, and end with dying 'of the burden of an honour unto which I was not born.'"

"You purposely misunderstand me! Who talks of compliments? who talks of honour? Oh, Ursula!" he cried, in great emotion, "do you not see how passionately I love you?"

"What!" she said. "A woman who finds virtue wearisome?"

"For heaven's sake don't recall those terrible words!—forget them—forget them, as I will!"

"What!" she continued, bitterly. "A woman who does not respect herself?"

"Yes! yes! and a thousand times yes, were it a thousand times true! Oh, child, could not you see that all my hate was love? where were your eyes that you did not see this? Where was your heart that you did not feel it? Why, child, at the very moment that you were uttering those horrid words my whole heart was going out in passionate adoration before you! God forgive me; I believe I adored the very words themselves! Don't you see that you have driven me mad— mad—mad!" and he threw himself at her feet in a paroxysm of passion.

"This is dreadful!" said Ursula, greatly shocked. "Pray, pray, Monsieur de Saldes, endeavour to control yourself——"

"I know," he answered, in the greatest agitation. "I beg your pardon—I have no right. See," he said, in broken accents, "I am quite calm now. Now tell me, I entreat of you, is there no hope? absolutely none? Tell me— only remember what it is that you are doing. If you reject me, you take away my last hope—my last anchor—the one thread by which I still hold to what is loveable and venerable in life."

"Do not ask it!" she said, in great trouble. "Monsieur de Saldes, I cannot marry you, for I cannot love you. And now, for heaven's sake, let us put an end to this painful interview; no earthly good can be gained by my staying here any longer—alas! what good has come of my staying so long? Good-night, Monsieur de Saldes——"

He had turned from her and sunk into a chair, and putting his arms on the table, laid his head down on them.

"Good-night, René," she said again. She spoke very gently, but her voice sounded hopelessly calm and composed. He, on the contrary, was shaken from head to foot by emotion. She went a step nearer to him, and stood for another instant waiting, but he did not speak nor lift his head, and like a ghost she passed noiselessly out of the room.

He remained in the same position for, I should think, nearly a quarter of an hour after she was gone, and I began to wonder if he would stay there all night, and what was to become of me. At last he gave a heavy sigh, got up, and went out into the garden through the conservatory, while I made a rush through the room and found myself in a second at the top of the staircase, with my heart beating like a great bell in my head and my ears, and all over my body.

I found Ursula walking up and down the room in a state of immense excitement.

"Did it ever happen to you to do a horribly painful thing that you knew was the only thing to do, and yet to feel all the while that in doing it you were shutting a stone down upon your heart for ever?" She stopped for a few seconds, then suddenly said, "René has asked me to marry him and I have refused." And covering her face with her hands she went into a passion of crying.

I took her in my arms and tried to soothe and comfort her; but nothing could calm her sorrow, nothing stop those tears that flowed and flowed until I thought the whole woman would turn, like Undine, into a stream before my face. I implored her to reconsider her decision, told her that I was sure she had been hasty—that a man who loved her as much as it was clear he did, would never abide by an answer given in a moment of excitement—that a word, a sign, a look would be sufficient to recall him. She suddenly looked up in my face with those curious heavy eyes of hers and said,—" You think I am crying because I have refused him ?—because I love him ? My dear, it is not that : I am crying because I love him no more. I loved him once with an agony of love : for four whole years I loved him, when he didn't care about me, and the fire is all burnt out; and (oh ! to think of it !) my heart was like a pinch of dry dust while he was lying at my feet. Oh ! isn't it shocking that it should all come too late, and that I should have nothing left here"—and she struck her heart repeatedly with a great distress—" but a stone—a stone !"

She then by degrees told me how when she was a child of fifteen he had renewed his acquaintance with her father at Florence and had become almost an inmate of their house. He was always passionately fond of music, it seems, and would come and pass hour after hour listening to her singing. It was then that she got attached to him ; but, by her account, all the passion was on her side, while nothing but his vanity was interested in the matter. "He played with me," she said, "exactly as a cat plays with a mouse. He never once committed himself in words during all those four years that he all but lived with us; but he used at times to indulge in tendernesses that sent me into a paradise of happiness, and then at other times he would seem to treat me only as a little child, and pass me over and neglect and desert me completely for a while. Then when my health used to give way, so that I could neither eat nor sleep any more, he would suddenly come, and cure me all in an instant with a look or a word that sent me on a ray of sunshine back into my poor fool's paradise again. What made it worse was, that at that very time there was a woman there—that Madame de Malan—whom he did really care about; and I went through tortures of jealousy when I was a mere child, that I can give you no idea of, and that were terribly bad for my whole nature and character. It was a dreadful double jealousy that swallowed up my whole existence for a time; for you must know that she had contrived to bewitch my father too—my poor father, who was no longer young,—and she took him too completely away from me. In my utter desolateness I used to cast myself down before God and pray by turns that my father might be left to me—that René might be left to me—that she might take one and leave me the other; but no, nothing short of both would satisfy that inexorable love of admiration."

"Was she so very attractive then?" said I.

"Oh, she was a wretched twopence of a woman, *disant assez bien la romance*, with a shivering shred of a voice : a miserable little creature with painted eyes, and as flat as a board!" Here she unconsciously gave a superb glance at herself in the looking-glass, and burst out laughing at her own vehemence, while the tears were still lying in bright drops on her face. "My little Venetian maid, who saw all the pain she caused me, and hated her for it, used to say of her :—' Mi no vedo sta beiezza. Non gha ne anca la radice di un petto!' In fact, she had no roots of any sort. She was made up of a morbid love of excitement at any price, and a restless vanity, unassuageable and pitiless, that, like the horseleech's daughter, was for ever crying,—' Give—give—give.' But I, too, am pitiless," she continued, looking at the clock. "You have to be up at three, and here am I preventing you from getting a chance of rest. Oh, do go to bed, Bessie!"

"But, my dear child," said I, "how long ago did all this happen?"

"Five years ago," she answered. "I am four-and-twenty now."

"And have you never felt any inclination for any one since then?"

"Never," she said. "I have tried once or twice to get up a sort of something for people who have cared for me; but it was all of no use! I turned sick and weary in the midst of my flirtation, and clapped a sudden extinguisher down upon the miserable farthing rushlight that it was. I'm burnt out, and there's an end of it! Oh, Bessie, get to bed. I am so ashamed of having troubled you with all this! Be sure you wake me up to bid me good-by."

She began trying to take the pins out of her hair, and to undress herself, but her hands shook so that she couldn't untie her strings; and so, much against her will, I put the poor child to bed. What an odd nature it was! She said after she had kissed me, as she turned her head on the pillow, "Don't trouble about me, dear Bess! I'm not worth it. I shall go in for ambition now, and marry a great duke. How pleased Lady Blankeney will be with the dear duchess!" She had hardly uttered the words before she was fast asleep. I stayed by her bedside for some minutes, looking at her face, which was as white as the sheet on which she lay, and at the black bar of her eyebrows, and at her long turned-up eyelashes, and then I lay down for an hour. At four I got up, and put on my things, and went once more softly to her bedside. She slept like a baby, and so I would not disturb her, but writing, "God bless you, dearest Ursula," on a slip of paper, left it on her pillow, and crept gently out of the room, and downstairs.

"Mademoiselle, la voiture est avancée," says the pasty, sleepy Hyacinthe.

I get in, I give a parting glance into the silver vapour that enshrouds the well-known landscape, the door is shut, and down the hill we go—through the gate; and thud—thud! over the wooden bridge with a sad heart, very unlike the anxious one that crossed the same water only a week ago; then across a bit of plain, starlit and mystical, that made me think of "Jacob's Dream" in the Dulwich

Gallery, and then suddenly into the dark night of the forest. My dear French friends, farewell!

A gray still passage, heaven dissolving itself in rain, and an arrival in London, dripping, dismal, black; but there on the platform stood William and mother, and dear old aunt Emily, waving a large red-silk pocket-handkerchief as we rolled into the station, and the next minute I was in their arms.

I was a whole week in London without hearing anything of Ursula, and was beginning to be a little afraid that her affection for me was not a real thing, and that she liked me less than she had fancied she did—when at last the long-expected missive arrived. Here it is:

"Hôtel Vouillemont, Rue des Champs Elysées, Paris.
"MY DEAREST BESSIE,—I receive at this very instant of time a letter from my agent at the Holt, informing me of the death of old Mr. Vaughan, the rector of my parish. This living, I rejoice to say, is in my gift, and I hope that Mr. L'Estrange will make me happy by accepting it. The living is worth six hundred a year, and there is a very pretty little house, the agent tells

me, exactly opposite one of the Holt gates. Ah, my dear Bess, do you remember the evening when we brushed our hair by the fire at Marny, and you told me about those sad eleven years (now really sad no more), and I could find nothing to say but 'good gracious!' The sound of my own voice saying these words has haunted me ever since. The fact was, that at that very time they had written to tell me that Mr. Vaughan was dangerously ill and eighty years old, and I was turning in my head the probability of his death, and the joy that it would be to me to offer the rectory to your William. But I dared say nothing, dear; for I have observed, as a general rule, that it's always the right people who die, and the wrong people who go recovering and living on for ever, when nobody wants them, and I was so dreadfully afraid the poor old thing might pick up again and disappoint me. I enclose a letter to Mr. L'Estrange, which you must give him from me, in which I make him a formal proffer of the living.

"Monsieur de Saldes went back to Paris before I came down that morning that you left. Dear Madame Olympe said that she was very glad of it, because he had evidently taken one of his violent antipathies to me, and that there was no fighting against these things. I feel rather glad, on the whole, to think that he will never be able to say of me, ' This, too, is vanity and vexation of spirit.'

"Jacques and I stayed on all Monday at Marny with Madame Olympe and Jeanne, and only came to Paris on Tuesday. I found Lady Blankeney crying in little showers all the day long. It seems that her dear Faubourg St. Germain countess was furious at having neither Jacques nor myself at her concert, and behaved very rudely, and not at all in the Faubourg St. Germain manner, to the poor woman—who in return is behaving as ill as anything so feeble can behave to me and Jacques. And so, dear, I suddenly cut adrift from her, went to an hotel of my own, and am coming over by myself. But as I suppose it wouldn't be quite possible for me to live alone and keep my character in your evil-thinking country, I propose that you should persuade Mrs. Hope to take charge of me, and give me the comfort of her kindness and the countenance of her respectability. I trust to you, dear Bess, to bring this plan to success. Do you think your mother would quite die of Jacques?

Both he and Giambattista have promised to come over and pay me a long visit at the Holt in the summer. She must set against that the delight of having you living next door to her. I shall be in London Thursday night. Meanwhile, and for ever, I am

"Your attached friend,
"URSULA HAMILTON."

What more is there to say? My marriage is fixed for the end of next month, and the day after to-morrow we all go down with our dear Portia to her northern Belmont. I have seen her reject the wrong casket—may she choose the right one when the time comes!

THE END.